Burned Out on Being Good

What to do if religion is wearing you out

Steven Mosley

Pacific Press® Publishing Association
Nampa, Idaho
Oshawa, Ontario, Canada

Edited by Glen Robinson
Designed by Robert Mason

Copyright © 1998 by
Pacific Press® Publishing Association
Printed in the United States of America
All Rights Reserved

Mosley, Steven R., 1952-
    Burned out on being good : what to do if your religion is wearing
you out / Steven Mosley.
        p.   cm.
    ISBN 0-8163-1578-7 (alk. paper)
    1. Christian life—Seventh-day Adventist authors.   2. Spiritual life—
Seventh-day Adventist authors.   I. Title.
BX6154.M65   1998
248.4'867—dc21   97-35337
                                                                              CIP

98 99 00 01 02 * 5 4 3 2 1

Contents

Standards:
Quantity Versus Quality

CHAPTER ONE

Are You Worn Out by the Weeds?

We stood on a very flat piece of Texas. The sun never blinked. And the occasional breeze that wandered by couldn't be bothered to keep us company. With our ragged tennis shoes, torn T-shirts, and unkempt hair, we were a pretty sorry crew.

Shean leaned on his hoe, staring down at three strands of wheat grass, and mumbled a complaint about no one bringing a radio. Harold began to knock the yellow flowers off dandelions, one by one. Jack was busy pummeling a scrawny, non-descript weed because several burs had gotten stuck to his pant leg. J.T. slowly circled a patch of clover, asking no one in particular whether it could be considered a legitimate part of the lawn.

We were five souls in the purgatory of an extended work program, earning tuition for our year at Valley Grande Academy. Hoeing weeds occupied our hours when there were no ditches to dig or garbage bins to dump. If all else failed, the boys could always be sent out after the weeds. So we'd meander over the campus with that looping shuffle of paid-by-the-hour peons, dragging our hoes behind us, find some dandelions and slowly begin bothering them to death.

There wasn't any realistic hope of eliminating all the weeds; our campus included several wide fields. We were just putting in time under a low, gray sky. By the time we straggled back to the dorm after eight hours of hoeing and hacking, every muscle was one long groan. It was a strange kind of exhaustion, different from the mellow tiredness that follows a long football game. This left us drained and numb. So after supper we just laid around and played cards or listened to our clandestine radios, feeling like old men.

One of the reasons I can't forget those hours is because in my mind they became a picture of the religious life. What do Christians *do* anyway? They hoe weeds. At least that's what it seemed to most of us at the academy. You have to keep fighting off the evils of the world that creep up around you.

Look out! There's a patch of lust springing up over there—and you know how fast that stuff grows. Whoa, here's a string of Satanism subtly infiltrating the church. Oh, and right under your feet there's a thorny cluster of doctrinal error. Better cut that down.

That was our picture of religious goodness. Hacking at weeds.

Take the Ping-Pong Ball Revival, for example. One year our school principal left on a week-long business trip and put the Bible teacher in charge. Pastor Fry decided this would be a good opportunity to spark a revival. How do you do it in seven days? Well, he met with the student counsel and pushed through some quick "reforms." Start with modesty in dress, surely a worthwhile goal. How do you ensure that the skirts are long enough and the pants aren't too tight? Why not have the girls kneel down in the dorm lobby each morning, where the dean can check to see if their hems reach the carpet. (This was the mini-skirt era.) Let's do that.

And the boys? Let's line them all up on the sidewalk and apply the Ping-Pong ball test. You slip Ping-Pong balls under their belts. If they drop all the way down to the shoelaces, the pants are OK, not too form-fitting.

Isn't it funny how styles change? Today, my son—on the way out the door with his skateboard—wears these incredibly baggy things. You could drive a pickup through his pant leg. He would have passed the test with flying colors. Our teachers fought a constant battle over hair creeping over our ears. My son's present teachers grow pale because he continually wants to shave the sides of his head.

Well, for some reason, the revival never did get off the ground. Maybe they couldn't get enough Ping-Pong balls. But as the thing fizzled out, one thought kept going through my head: There's got to be more to it than this.

It wasn't that Pastor Fry was a hard-nosed legalist. As a matter of fact, he was one of the most likable teachers on campus. But in that religious culture, when people cast around for a way to be good, the only thing they could think of was *hoeing weeds*, stamping out a few shoots of worldliness.

That's our job as Christians, isn't it? After all, we can't just let sin take over our lives. We have to keep at it. The dark, fertile soil of carnality and worldliness is always threatening, always throwing up weeds.

And that's the rub. You never really have any hope of getting them all. You no sooner hack away at one thing than another is growing like crazy somewhere else. After a while, you start wondering what the point is. You get tired of just working by the hour, just hoeing weeds. Why not roll around in them for a while?

In chapel services at the school, we heard a lot about how wonderful the Christian life was—transforming power available to one and all. But nothing we saw around us matched the rhetoric. The words were so big, the promises so extravagant. Why then did religion have to feel so small?

None of us thought we could fit into it. And that made that scraggly line of weed-hoers out there in the wide fields quite wary of the Big Man Upstairs. Shean was a bit older than the rest of us and had been through some pretty tough times. He was sure that a little dark cloud followed him everywhere. I expressed skepticism. But once, after supper, we were walking across campus when he pointed up. Sure enough, a little dark cloud was following him. Shean suspected that God played favorites.

J.T. wanted to "expand his mind" in other directions. He wasn't sure what that meant. He was just sure he didn't want his life confined to the pages of our church manual. Harold was too amiable to question the Almighty. But he had no intentions of "getting under His thumb" anytime soon.

Sometimes we'd meet people who wanted to do more than hoe weeds; people who made a big deal about religion. But they were such a peculiar breed. They always seemed to wear dark slacks and starched white shirts. They spoke a lot in King James English and appeared to be on intimate terms with the beasts of Revelation. Every encounter with these people turned into something awkward. Their religious goodness seemed wrapped around them as tightly as packing wire.

My roommate Jack had once been confronted with "what the Holy Spirit could do to you" at a school in the mountains specializing in 24-hour-a-day-holiness—and he was still running. A lanky, shy, kid, he seemed to be laboring against a divine law that stretched from horizon to horizon. There was no escape from its endless requirements.

But he did his best to defend himself. Each Sabbath, Jack faithfully carried a miniature pack of poker cards to church in his inside coat pocket. If a sermon hit a little bit too close to home, he would reach in and finger the ace of spades or queen of hearts. The poker cards were his security, preventing the angels from getting too close.

The unspoken commitment in our dorm was: leave religion alone as much as possible. For some reason, I clung to the belief that there must be something more to God than what we were getting. There just *had* to be.

But we didn't find it. Most of my peers laid aside their hoes a long time ago.

J.T. shattered his mind on extended drug trips.

Shean found employment as projectionist in a porn theatre, moving as far away from purity as physically possible.

My roommate Jack wanted more than anything else to belong to a fast car. After all, he had to keep looking over his shoulder to see if fanaticism was gaining on him. He died in a head-on collision.

Harold didn't turn against the faith in any obvious way. He just began moving in other circles, making sure that it kept a respectable distance.

I am still haunted by those faces that stare back at me from my academy yearbook. I see so many casualties, so many people who burned out trying to be good. And I still lament the fact that Christianity appeared to be an exhausting one-way street for them.

The religion of avoidance

One of the pitfalls of a legalistic culture is that sooner or later it creates a religion of avoidance. Our faith comes to be defined by the things we avoid. That's one big reason so many people burn out on being good.

We seem to confront a world full of threats: crude rock lyrics blaring out on the airwaves, suggestive TV shows on every station, riotous parties in every neighborhood, secular humanists behind every institution. The easiest sermon to preach is one on why the world is going to hell. The quickest religious bestseller is one that red-letters a new hidden danger out there threatening the faith.

When "being good" is a matter of continually whittling life down to proper size—eliminating the weeds—then it's going to seem quite pale and stifling. Life has huge potential for good or ill, so our preoccupations with jewelry, foul language, and whether you should raise your hands in church or not don't seem very earth-shaking to a lot of people. We get tangled up in our particular denominational brand of rule-making. We have to build ever higher, ever stricter, barriers against the dandelions, ragweeds, and crabgrass of the world that keep threatening to take over the church's immaculate lawns.

Always having to say No burns people out. You always have to be on guard. Weeds are popping up everywhere. Trying to get them all wears people down; it's simply not sustainable.

A religion of avoidance manages to be both intimidating and unchallenging at the same time. The thought of spending your life always vigilant, guarding against those little sins, fills people with dismay. It's just too hard not to fall. And yet, though terribly difficult, the prospect doesn't arise as a great challenge either; it doesn't seem worthy of life's best energies.

The religion of avoidance sometimes becomes animistic. Animism is a primitive religion that affirms that good and evil spirits inhabit all kinds of objects. In certain cultures, for example, parents may warn their young children about a certain kind of tree as a source of moral peril. Or they may point out certain stones as objects of blessing.

Christians are not animists. We do believe that we live in a spiritual world and in the midst of a conflict between good and evil. But it's important to remember that most *things* aren't good or evil. Holiness is not primarily a matter of getting bad things out of our lives.

Adventists (and many other conservative Christians), however, too often try to do just that. Movies are bad. Rock-and-roll is bad. Certain words are bad. Tattoos are bad. Heavy and tight skirts are bad.

All kinds of things can be abused, of course. And some things lend themselves to abuse much more than others. But when we concentrate on things, we're dealing with the wrong end of the stick. It's *people* who have moral problems, not things. Many movies major in gratuitous violence and sex. But I don't think anyone would want to launch a campaign against books, because many books major in gratuitous violence and sex.

In the religion of avoidance, certain styles of dress or music or worship take on moral or immoral weight. This keeps us from looking at the things of the heart that really defile human beings. Abusive anger, egotism, insensitivity—these are dangers to beware, these are things that defile us. When we just focus on the terrible things out there that are going to come in and defile us, we're not fighting the real battle. We're just subsisting on a religion of avoidance.

Where is the place for experiment and risk in such a defensive lifestyle? How can people grow as human beings if they're constantly worried about "creeping worldliness"? In the religion of avoidance, the pious see some thin entering wedge—something that could possibly lead to something evil—everywhere.

Teenagers get the usual warning: Paying too much attention to the opposite sex can lead to spending time in their company, which can lead to hand-holding, which can lead to kissing, which can lead to embracing, which can lead to petting, which leads to sex. In this scenario, every gesture of affection becomes one more step down that slippery slope to perdition.

Instead of helping kids use their minds and hearts, instead of encouraging kids to practice self-control and helping them understand what's appropriate and what's not appropriate in various relationships, we demonize the physical.

Nothing sends a chill down the spines of those caught up in the religion of avoidance like mere "amusements." Frequenting bowling alleys could lead to hanging out at pool halls, which could lead to smoking, which could lead to drugs. Associating with the "wrong kind of people" could lead to talking like them and thinking like them. Checking out a book or a TV program that's "just entertainment" could soften the brain, which could cloud our thoughts, which could make us incapable of taking in the solid food of the Word and render us helpless before the ceaseless brain-washing of the devil.

Church members are warned: listening to that non-Adventist evangelist on television could lead you into spiritual seduction. You might start speaking in tongues and fall captive to the counterfeit Holy Spirit.

Of course it's possible to be swept up by some cultic teaching—especially if you're emotionally vulnerable. Of course it's possible to waste away your life going from one amusement to another. But the religion of avoidance tends to see everything that is not explicitly religious as explicitly bad. There's the church—this particular church—and there's the world. Everything in the church is good. Everything in the world is bad.

The truth is there's every conceivable kind of good and bad both in the church and in the world. There are "secular" books that ennoble the soul. There are extremely religious books that promote a dysfunctional view of life. There are feature films that glamorize violence. There are feature films that make you ache inside because life is so precious. Some religious television reduces Jesus to salesmanship. Some religious television shows Jesus as a compelling Saviour.

There are symphonies that make you feel someone understands your deepest longings. There are pop songs that perfectly express the precise romantic moment you stand in and make you want to inhabit that moment forever. There's rock-and-roll that plugs in all your energy. There are ballads that massage your heart.

Every kind of great, good, mediocre and bad art exists in the world. You can't just put things in boxes labeled "amusement" and store them away out of sight. You have to have discernment. You have to develop sensitivity. What blesses me and inspires me at this particular time may turn you off. What warms you in your particular emotional state may leave me cold.

Sometimes laughing your head off on a roller coaster is an escape from problems you should be dealing with. Sometimes laughing your head off on a roller coaster is the perfect way to express the exuberance about life that's welling up from your toes.

People need some measure of security if they are to grow in a healthy way. They need to know that there's plenty of good out there to experience, as well as bad to avoid. It's unhealthy to grow up always afraid that every little misstep will just lead to another and another and another until you end up helpless in the clutches of the Enemy.

Out there hoeing weeds under the big Texas sun, I imagined that there was more to religion than that—there *had* to be more, there *had* to be something healthier. But what exactly was the alternative? I didn't have a hint of what it could be until Bill Shelly came into our world of miniature rights and wrongs.

I met him the summer I started working at a furniture factory run by our academy. The first thing that struck me about Bill was that he worked rather cheerfully. I was hammering dresser drawer guides on a jig, going through the identical motions for eight hours. He was stuck in the paint room at the end of the assembly line, a pretty noxious place that left you feeling lightheaded at the end of the day. But Bill painted dressers and cabinets, grinning all the while as if he wasn't all there. And it wasn't just the fumes. He was alert, but somehow not at all trapped in that gloomy factory. I had this sense that he'd been places—and not just geographical ones.

Bill was sincere but never pretentious. We noticed he said grace at meals, and once in a while he talked about something he'd learned from the Bible. But he never wore a starched white shirt or talked King James English. That was a new trick. Bill was the first peer I had ever known who was both spiritual and normal, the first person who made religious goodness seem attractive.

I remember the evening it hit me. I was walking back to the dorm from supper and caught traces of purple, orange, and magenta flaring across the sky. Our horizon had always been rather dull—no dramatic landscape to speak of. And that summer the flat earth seemed always matched by that low gray sky. But on this evening the whole hemisphere was lighted up; the sky seemed enormous. I had not noticed sunsets much before. But this was quite a phenomenon. I'd never seen so much color in one place.

And as I looked west toward the dazzling sun, I noticed Bill sitting alone out on the football field bleachers. He had a book open on one knee. A bit of sunset reflected off the white pages. He was out there with his Bible, enjoying the dramatic sky. And I remembered it was a Friday evening, about the time when they dragged us into the chapel for vespers.

I stopped in my tracks. No one had told Bill he had to do this.

There were no rules in the school handbook saying you had to read your Bible on the bleachers every Friday evening. He was making something happen on his own, maybe his own version of vespers. He wasn't just putting in time, hoeing weeds.

Maybe he was even looking for God out there. And the wild idea struck me that religion could be an adventure. Maybe it could be as eloquent as that sunset. Maybe it could come out of your heart and mind instead of being imposed from the outside.

Bill seemed to be at ease out there, leaning back with his arms spread on the banch behind him. After staring a long, long time, I made my way slowly toward the bleachers.

CHAPTER TWO

Where Is Your Identity?

I gradually was to learn an important principle from Bill and others like him. One of the main reasons people burn out on being good and get stuck hoeing weeds is that they lose the most basic, the most essential, part of healthy religion. And that is seeking God.

The book of Romans is the classic document of Christian theology. In that epistle, Paul presents the basic problem all human beings share, and he presents the solution Jesus Christ created at the cross. It's interesting how he defines our essential problem:

> There is no one righteous, not even one;
> there is no one who understands,
> no one who seeks God.
> All have turned away . . . (Romans 3:10-12).

The basic flaw of human nature is this: we don't seek God. And this problem persists, even among people who are very religious.

In the Old Testament the prophets call over and over to the chosen: "Seek the Lord! Seek the Lord and live!"

Many churched individuals will do almost anything except seek God.

Serve on the nominating committee, teach earliteens, study doctrine—everything except pursue the essential relationship.

Bill out on the bleachers at sunset gave me a picture of what healthy religion is all about. I could not articulate the answer at the time. It didn't all register. But I had a glimpse: healthy religion is a way of seeking God that expands human life.

That's essential: a desire to get to know God on a personal level. It's amazing how often that gets lost in the shuffle of religious activity.

There's something that happens to religious people when we don't have this spiritual momentum of seeking God. And it happens over and over again. If our lives are not centered around this pursuit, they begin to center around something else: sin. It's not that we're sinning all the time. No, we're pointing out sin, glaring at sin, trying to avoid sin, shaking our finger at sin. Sin is the great enemy. But sin remains at the center of attention.

When it comes to expressing your religious faith, if you don't start with something you want to say about God, you always fall back on hoeing weeds; you always fall back on simply attacking sin. That's why people keep getting stuck in the religion of avoidance. And that kind of religion isn't sustainable in any healthy way. Always having to say No burns people out.

Pursuing hidden treasure

We need an alternative. We need a way of seeking God that expands our lives. When you want to know what healthy religion is really like, it's always useful to ask "What did Jesus say the kingdom of Heaven is like?" For example, look at this picture from Matthew 13:44: "The kingdom of heaven is like treasure hidden in a field. When a man found it, he hid it again, and then in his joy went and sold all he had and bought that field."

Here we have a man getting rid of his worldly possessions. He sold everything. Why? In order to avoid the love of money? In order to make a big sacrifice? No, he wanted very badly to get this hidden treasure; it was worth selling out for. In his *joy* he went out and sold all he had.

We successfully get rid of the bad, avoid evil, by pursuing something good, something better. We're in hot pursuit of a relationship with Jesus Christ and so we get rid of stuff that gets in the way. That is healthy religion. You get less of the world, because you want more of God.

Yes, we do have to avoid evil in this life. But people burn out on being good if avoidance is at the center of their religious life.

There's another thing that happens when seeking God is not at the center of our religion. Superficial things rush in to fill the vacuum. If we aren't intently pursuing a great God, religious goodness always shrinks into pettiness. We concentrate on little sins. When you're out hoeing weeds, you know what happens. You find the easiest weeds to hoe, the weakest dandelions to attack.

When we don't seek a big God, we become very concerned about little things.

People attack Christmas trees. Why, they were once part of pagan rites; we're bringing the devil into our homes! Hack, hack.

People get offended if someone raises their hands in church. Those who haven't cracked a smile in twenty years speak fearfully of unbridled emotionalism.

People wage great battles over the types of musical instruments used in worship. Horrors, we're turning church into a nightclub by using an electronic keyboard!

If you have something you want to express from your heart, something to say to God, then it doesn't much matter what kind of instruments they're using or where the words are. You want to praise your Lord. But if you have nothing to say, then all these details become very, very important. There's only one way to worship.

In my own case, if I'm really admiring something about God, then I can praise Him even through nineteenth century hymns that talk about "billows of love" and "hearts with rapture thrilled." But if I'm spiritually numb, with little to express, then I'll probably be griping about those boring hymns.

It certainly helps to be able to worship through a kind of music that you enjoy, that speaks to your heart. But other styles of worship don't have to bend you out of shape—if you have something to say.

Individuals who have nothing inside to express will cling desperately to the routine, the ritual, the way it's always been done. Churches that are decimated by back-stabbing, criticism, and factions take a firm stand on commandments such as: special music shall always come after the pastoral prayer.

If you have nothing great to pursue, you'll always cling to the small stuff, the petty stuff. You'll always go back to hoeing weeds.

Standards and identity

This issue of seeking God—of pursuing God—has a lot to do with our identity, both as individuals and as members of a church. It has everything to do with how we create a healthy identity—and how we select healthy "standards."

Many people in the Adventist Church fear we are losing our identity, or more precisely, they fear our identity is slipping away bit by bit. They look around at congregations and see distressing signs of the erosion of our "distinctive standards."

Adventists used to have a certain "look," something different from people "in the world." But now the lady teaching your kids in cradle roll wears bright red lipstick and more and more earrings seem to be cropping up in the pews, not just on the ears of visitors but on deaconesses and Sabbath School superintendents.

We used to be able to make very clear statements about jewelry, but now the whole issue—from broach to pin to bracelet to necklace—seems to be getting fuzzy.

Adventists used to uniformly avoid movie theaters and any place where dancing occurred. Hollywood glamorized everything that we thought decadent. And dancing seemed just a few steps removed from illicit sex. Not so long ago even pool halls and bowling alleys seemed breeding places of vice.

But now the deacons talk in the foyer about the latest Arnold Schwarzenegger movie, and even the pastor's wife has an opinion on whether Brad Pitt is a better actor than John Travolta. Now dancing seems like a perfectly normal thing to many of our academy kids.

Once all Adventists regarded rock-and-roll as a foreign tongue which, though almost incomprehensible, surely had no honorable intentions. Now the "contemporary Christian music" that's creeping into worship services seems to be speaking that language loud and clear.

Once we were known not just for never eating pork but for a very distinct health message. Many conscientious Adventists even avoided things like mayonnaise and catsup. Now it seems many of us are wolfing down hamburgers at Wendy's and McDonalds along with everybody else "in the world."

Once you could be assured that Adventists all over the world would be engaged in basically the same activities on Sabbath afternoons: taking nature walks, visiting the sick, reading the *Adventist Review*. Now all kinds of borderline amusements seem to be crowding into our Sabbaths. A soccer game in the park here, a "really good" movie on TV there, and pretty soon the seventh day becomes just another day off.

We used to go out Ingathering every fall. It was a rite of passage for many adolescents who had to go door to door asking neighbors to fill cans with dollar bills. Now we just write a check and get it over with.

Our standards are slipping. That's a common lament among the faithful in the pews. What is happening to Adventists? Are we becoming just like everyone else? A lot of people are wondering these days. We seem to be losing our identity. How can we get it back? It's an important question.

It's a question a young woman named Frances faced shortly after becoming a Seventh-day Adventist. She had accepted her first teaching job at a grade school in Virginia and began attending a church there.

After a few weeks, Frances realized that there were really two congregations in this church: those who sat on the right side and those who sat on the left.

Those on the right dressed very simply in clothes that were slightly out of date. The women never wore makeup of any kind. They never ate out on Sabbath and thought it preferable to walk to church than to drive. These individuals seemed to draw their identity from a strict adherence to standards: everything from what they ate to what they didn't do on the seventh day. Nothing was going to pollute their bodies or the Sabbath.

Those on the left didn't seem to emphasize these standards as much. They sometimes ate out after church. They sometimes ate meat. They seemed more "worldly" in general.

Frances was still glowing from her discovery of Adventism. The "27 Fundamental Beliefs" still buzzed inside the head of this very idealistic young woman. So naturally she thought those on the left were simply a lesser version of the real church members on the right.

But something struck her when she attended their respective potlucks. The "real Adventists" just couldn't stop putting down those on the other side of the church as they chewed on their cutlets and cole slaw. They seemed to have a need to keep pointing out where others fell short of their standards.

However, the "lesser Adventists" on the left seemed much more friendly and open at their potlucks. They didn't feel compelled to put anyone down or defend their particular standards.

Frances found that she loved to visit in the homes of these people and discuss all kinds of things. That just didn't seem possible in the homes of the "real Adventists." They were too uptight about preserving their religious security through strict behavior.

What Frances found early on in her Adventist life was a rather distressing paradox. She wanted to be a "real Adventist." She wanted to follow God's principles all the way. And yet she didn't want to become like those who did. Something was wrong.

The problem Frances encountered was that those who seemed to champion strict standards were really stuck in the religion of avoidance. Their standards revolved around what they avoided. And something always happens in this kind of religion of externals: You start identifying yourself by what you avoid—I don't drink; I don't dance; I don't play around.

That's your identity: *what you don't do.* And you try to protect that identity by putting down those who don't measure up. An identity based on what you avoid is fundamentally unhealthy. It leads to burnout.

Identifying yourself by what you don't do eventually leads to identifying yourself by what you're not: Well, at least I'm not a charismatic, rolling in the aisles, talking gibberish. I'm not a Roman Catholic seeing the Virgin Mary in a tortilla. I'm not a New-Ager fondling crystals.

This is identity based on a vacuum, based on avoidance. When we go down this road, we can end up as dry as the Pharisee in the temple praying: I thank You, Lord, that I am not as this publican.

So what does this imply about "standards"? Should we just throw them out altogether? Should we just ignore external behavior?

I think Frances shows us a better alternative.

She didn't really find a way out of her dilemma until she began to meet a greater variety of believers. It happened later in her career as a college teacher. One of her fellow professors made things very clear.

Herb Roth served as the chairperson of the English Department at Southwestern Adventist College for many years, while his wife, Irene, worked as the college registrar.

Frances had gone through a very difficult period in her life when she began teaching at SAC, and she needed solid, accepting Christian friends. The Roths proved to be heaven sent. When she went over to their house for supper, she always came back refreshed, even on days that had begun in loneliness and discouragement.

Frances never heard these people utter a word of criticism about another human being—quite a feat in an inbred Adventist community like Keene's. She never saw them act in an unkind way toward another individual. They were always there to assist people in need. They were always helping out, very quietly, in the church in some way. Herb and Irene were the kind of people you are just glad to have around.

What struck Frances about them most was that, although they practiced very high standards, their identity was not wrapped up in their standards. Proper behavior wasn't the focus of their spiritual life. They emphasized something else: the devotional life, getting to know Jesus. As Herb put it, "You can't look at people; you have to look at Christ."

Frances didn't imagine that the Roths had ever been to a movie in their lives. But she felt comfortable talking with them about the movies she'd seen. They were good listeners. They were also strict vegetarians. But they didn't talk much about their diet.

Herb wasn't a Bible scholar, but people enjoyed the Sabbath School class he taught very much. He just knew the Bible, and he knew the Person behind it.

Frances saw something very real in these people that sustained her during a period of doubt and disaffection with the church. I'm very glad that Frances found a way out of her dilemma. Because this woman became my mother and was able to nurture in me a healthy desire to know Jesus Christ as a friend.

Building our identity through a person

What makes people like Herb and Irene Roth different from the people on the right side of that church in Virginia? Both of them adhere to what most of us would call high Adventist standards. But the individuals in Virginia tried to get their identity from those strict standards. The Roths got it somewhere else.

As we've seen, the alternative to the religion of avoidance is a religion that pursues something good, a religion that seeks God. Similarly, the alternative to trying to build an identity on what you avoid is to build an identity on your relationship with Jesus Christ.

This should be a fairly obvious point. So why do many people get stuck in the religion of avoidance—even though it's a dead end, even though it leads steadily to burnout?

Because they have no alternative.

Few individuals decide that their identity as human beings will be tied to how closely they follow dietary laws in Leviticus or how boring they make the Sabbath. This only happens by default. It only happens because there seems no other way. It only happens because people are trying to fill up a hole inside them.

When you don't have nurturing relationships, you look for other things to take their place. Secular people may try to get a flashier car or a bigger house or a fancier title. They may try to find security in those substitutes.

Religious people do this in other ways. They try to have higher standards than their neighbors. It's not that they're stupid. It's not that they wouldn't like to have a nurturing relationship with God. It's that they haven't been able to find such a relationship. For whatever reasons, it's just not happening.

If you haven't experienced loving nurture in your life, you probably don't feel close to God. You don't feel His love. You don't feel accepted. And so what do you do to fight the terrible insecurity that inevitably wraps itself around you? You have to settle for the alternative: being stricter than your neighbor. That's the only way you have of feeling *in*. You can't come up with the gracious qualities that naturally result from a nurturing relationship with God. So you have to settle for strict behavior. That's the only thing you can produce. And you imagine that if you can just produce enough of it, you will be accepted, loved, secure.

Seeking your identity in your standards is a big mistake. And it's a mistake that the church, unfortunately, can play a part in. Instead of recognizing the constant harping on external standards as a symptom of spiritual emptiness, we *admire* it, we *promote* it. It's supposed to be a way of saving our church, of getting us back to our pure roots. We don't realize that all too often it's the road to burnout.

Curiously enough, talk of "standards" hardly ever seems to dwell on things like kindness, sensitivity, and patience. But aren't those things "standards" that should characterize the follower of Christ?

The person walking around without a religious instinct in his body can always dress a certain way, listen to a certain kind of music, talk a certain jargon, eat certain foods. He can look and sound like a member of a certain religious culture. But is that godliness?

What we have to be careful of is centering our religious lives around things that only *simulate* holiness. Things that create a certain religious appearance shouldn't be confused with the real thing. We can work long and hard; we can build up all kinds of walls against evil—and still end up just simulating holiness.

What we call standards can certainly be meaningful for individuals. A person who abused drugs for years and associates a certain kind of rock music with that addiction may throw out all his CDs when he becomes a Christian. It's a meaningful gesture on his part. But that doesn't make him holy or healthy. It's the qualities that Christ is nurturing in his heart that make the difference.

A young woman who associates a certain style of clothing with her previously promiscuous life may change her whole wardrobe when she becomes a Christian. That's a statement she needs to make. But it's not her religion. Jesus creating fruits of the Spirit is her religion.

Other people without an encounter with Christ can change the music they listen to or the clothes they wear until they're blue in the face, but still only simulate holiness. Nothing has really happened.

Standards can be a symptom of internal change. But they're the symptom, not the real thing.

The strictness of our standards alone is not the issue. Yes, sometimes people who are less and less strict in their behavior are losing ground spiritually. And yes, sometimes people who are more and more strict in their behavior are masking a spiritual emptiness inside.

But these behaviors are ymptoms. The real problem and the real solution revolve around our identity. Where is it? Being strict because you love Jesus is a good thing. Being strict because that's your only source of security is a bad thing.

We will never find a secure identity in what we avoid. We'll never find a secure identity in what we're not. We'll only find it in a nurturing relationship—when we reach out and actually touch the Living God.

It was one of those long Sabbath days I endured as a youth. I was slouched in a back pew following a worship service, wondering, as usual, why church had to be so boring. The feeble organ music had finally trickled away altogether. Why did the religious life seem to attract mainly the old, I wondered, those who didn't have the energy to sin? I cast a disapproving eye on the smattering of old ladies in the church. They'd been warbling all the hymns; I imagined they had nothing better to do. They were all sitting in a line, one behind the other, down the left side of the aisle—the better, no doubt, to slip quickly to the lobby afterward and start gossiping.

I was identifying myself by what I was not: I thank God that I am not as these old women.

One man, a stocky gentleman sitting alone near the front of the church, lingered too. No one had sat in his pew. There, I imagined, was someone as isolated as myself. Nothing in the service seemed to have touched him either.

The grandmother-types seated by the aisle in the rows behind him also waited with heads bowed in the silence. The lone man finally rose from his seat, fumbled for a book, and stuck it under his arm. It was an oversized volume. And I realized, looking at the man's sunken eyes, that the book was thick with Braille lettering. He turned to make his way rather clumsily toward the rear of the sanctuary.

Immediately the old woman just behind him reached out and clasped his hands tightly. They exchanged a few animated words. He stepped forward, and the next lady at the aisle reached for his hands in greeting, then the next. Each woman beamed as she said his name and expressed her delight in seeing him.

I realized that in this way the ladies had formed an unobtrusive escort, passing him from hand to hand, guiding his steps to the foyer. And he wasn't being led along like some lost child; he was carried along joyfully. As he came closer, the man's face transfixed me. Around those glazed eyes his features shouted joy. Even I could see that the old women's feeble, wrinkled hands had really touched him.

I was sitting there identifying myself by what I excluded, by what I was not; they were showing me what God is like:

> I led them with cords of human kindness,
> with ties of love;
> I lifted the yoke from their neck (Hosea 11:4).

Those women had something to say, something wonderful to tell me about God. He longs to reach out and make contact with us. And it's not just to make sure that we take the correct steps and go in the right direction. He wants to share His warmth with us, His joy in our companionship. He wants to greet us as a friend, not just lead us along like a lost child. Because it's only in that warmth that we can go in the right direction. It's only as we find our identity in Him that we can walk as children of light.

CHAPTER THREE

A Faith That Expands Us

Healthy religion follows a natural process of growth. That's something people burning out on being good desperately need to know. They need to know that the opposite of the religion of avoidance is not some other frantic pursuit; it's not some other compulsion. It's a response to love.

Unhealthy religion is a response to guilt and dysfunction. Healthy religion is a response to love. The opposite of burning out on being good is growing up on being loved. Here's how it happens.

First, you center your religion on simply wanting to get to know God better, on seeking God, on pursuing God.

Then as you get to know this God and deepen a friendship with Jesus Christ, you develop a secure identity *in* Jesus Christ. The relationship tells you who you are. The love and acceptance you are receiving tell you—on an experiential level—that you are cherished as a child of God.

So, as an extension of that relationship, you start wanting to express love back. You are discovering how compassionate and gracious and faithful this God really is. You now have something great to say about God, to express about God. So you are motivated to act in compassionate and gracious and faithful ways.

A religion of qualities

This process creates what we might call a religion of qualities. Healthy religion is a religion of qualities—like love, joy, and peace. That is the end result of knowing God. You are absorbing God's good qualities—His love and grace— and so you have qualities to give. You have to receive in order to give. You have to have something great you want to express about God. Having something to say from the heart is what produces the fruits of the Spirit.

This is an expansive process. This is not about whittling life down to proper size. It's about expanding—from the inside out.

What is healthy religion like? Look at what Jesus says the kingdom of heaven is like. Look at Matthew 13:31, 32, for example. "The kingdom of heaven is like a mustard seed, which a man took and planted in his field. Though it is the smallest of all your seeds, yet when it grows, it is the largest of garden plants and becomes a tree, so that the birds of the air come and perch in its branches."

The tiny seed expands under the broad sky, growing into a plant so large that, as Matthew says, birds can nest in its branches.

The more we concentrate on the essential seed, on knowing God, the more expansive our religious life becomes. The less we concentrate on knowing God, the more constricted our religious life becomes.

So we need to ask ourselves a question: What best characterizes our religion? Is our spirituality (or lack thereof) determined more by what we pursue or by what we avoid? What occupies the center of our attention? What requires our greatest energies? Pursuing or avoiding?

God doesn't want our religion to shrink us into avoidance or pettiness. He wants to expand our lives with His positive qualities. He wants us to nurture that good tree spreading its branches against the sky.

Fill your minds, he says, with "whatever is true, whatever is Noble . . . whatever is admirable—if anything is excellent or praiseworthy—think about such things" (Philippians 4:8).

Don't just curse the darkness. "Live as children of light (for the fruit of the light consists in all goodness, righteousness and truth)" (Ephesians 5:8, 9). It's a big world out there under the blazing sky. There's room to stretch all kinds of branches, create all kinds of fruit.

If any man is in Christ, he is a new creature (2 Corinthians 5:17, NASB). How wide can you get? Healthy religion creates a whole new creation.

Healthy religion isn't about putting square pegs in square holes. It's about expanding our lives. Healthy religion isn't just a matter of being more religious. It's a matter of "attaining to the whole measure of the fullness of Christ" (Ephesians 4:13).

The religion of avoidance, the religion of legalism, by contrast, is drawn like a magnet to quantities. People without a religion of the heart need something to measure, some way to gauge their performance. How many proper activities have they engaged in this week? How many improper activities have they avoided? Quantities predominate.

It's something of a paradox, but people try to do a lot in the religious life often because they can do so little. Trust and compassion were out of reach for the Pharisees, but tithing mint, dill, and cumin, and ritually cleansing every cup and dish, were doable. So they did a lot of it. Mercy and sensitivity are still out of reach for some believers today, but dressing a certain way and talking a certain way and listening only to certain kinds of music are doable. So they do a lot of it. They can simulate holiness.

The only way to be more religious in this system is to increase the quantity: you do more or you avoid more things. You do more and more until you burn out. Or, if you have an iron will, you keep doing more until you can't move anymore; until you die.

I'll never forget the manI met who has experienced in his own family the dramatic difference between a religion of qualities and a religion of quantities.

He sat behind his desk rubbing his chin, a successful media executive in his early sixties, recalling what it was like to grow up Adventist. His responses to my questions, though polite and articulate, carried an edge.

Frank still felt some loyalty toward the church. But every once in a while some bitter remark would break through.

He believed the Adventist system was plagued "by this notion that you have to earn the divine smile. That's a horrible way to live. It's a plague of the Adventist system."

He despised people whose terrifying prophetic scenarios "hold people hostage to the end times." Even though the man was quite health conscious himself and didn't eat meat, he waved off the Adventist health message with a "baloney on all that vegetarian nonsense."

I wondered what was really behind these remarks. So he told me a story. And it became evident, as he told it, that the incident was still vivid in his mind.

He had just returned from a trip to Russia, shortly after the collapse of the Soviet Union, and he'd been quite moved by the way the people were responding to the gospel, which was being freely proclaimed after a half decade of religious oppression. The experience revitalized Frank's faith.

Frank went up to the Northwest for a family get-together with his siblings and his Adventist parents. He had a lot he wanted to share with them. As he was describing the interesting people he'd met and the exotic food he'd sampled, Frank's father, Richard, wanted to know, "You didn't eat meat over there, did you?"

Frank replied that he had no idea what some of the food he'd tasted was.

Richard straightened in his chair. He was a tough Montana rancher who'd worked hard all his life and boasted jet-black hair into his seventies. With a crooked grin on his weathered face, he announced, "Frankie, let me tell you this. No flesh food has crossed these lips in more than sixty years."

As a rowdy young man given to drink, Richard had been converted to uprightness by an Adventist evangelist. He was proud that he'd given up everything—drinking, smoking, coffee, movies, meat—just like that. He determined to serve God if it killed him.

And Richard had faithfully avoided these things for six decades.

Frank grinned back resignedly and said, "That's good, Dad."

A few moments later, Richard turned to his wife and said, "Mom, get me some juice from the kitchen."

She continued talking to her daughter for a few more seconds.

Richard exploded. He began berating his wife in front of their grown children. "What's the matter with you, woman? You just gonna sit there all day?"

Frank felt the blood rush to his head as he listened to his father's angry tirade. His mother, Margy, was the sweetest person he'd ever known; everybody loved her. It was outrageous that she had to put up with abuse like that from her husband.

That scene would haunt Frank for years. The father who wouldn't let meat touch his lips could spit out ugly words at the slightest provocation. The man had a strong will. He could say No to all kinds of things. But he had a hard time saying Yes to kindness or grace.

Frank admitted that his father probably never knowingly violated an Adventist prohibition during his life as a church member. The Sabbath remained undefiled; he would no more go into a store to buy something on Saturday than fly to the moon. But he did seem to spend many Sabbath hours rabidly criticizing those who were less punctilious than he was.

When Frank recalled his father's religion, it was the quantity of things he did or didn't do that stood out. What he remembered about his mother, Margy, however, were qualities of the heart.

Frank's voice softened as he described a trip he'd taken with her to visit some friends she hadn't seen in years. He was overwhelmed by the love these people expressed for his mother. There was Ruby, whom she had befriended as a young, pregnant Okie, alone in a new town in Oregon. This woman still regarded Margy as dearly as if she'd always been her mother. And there was the recovering alcoholic who murmured, "Aunt Margy, you're the most beautiful person I've ever known."

Margy had grown up in a religion environment that emphasized grace. Her faith was much simpler than her husband's; she was sustained by—" Jesus loves me, this I know." But her qualities of compassion had obviously changed lives.

In Frank's mind the quantity of his father's religion stood in sharp contrast with the quality of his mother's.

It's important to remember that people don't choose a religion of quantity. It chooses them. It's the only alternative for people who are empty inside. They can't come up with love, joy, peace, and kindness. So they have to come up with something else. When you don't have qualities, you have to compete with quantity.

People can avoid, say, catsup and mayonnaise for good reasons. People can also avoid catsup and mayonnaise because they desperately need to do more than their fellow believer who is merely vegetarian.

People can avoid roller-blading on the Sabbath for good reasons. People can also avoid roller-blading because their fellow believer doesn't and they have to avoid more things than him or her.

The religion of qualities is expansive, open-ended. The religion of quantities is a one-way street to exhaustion.

The religion of quantities debates long and hard about just when a brooch becomes a piece of adornment.

The religion of qualities finds new ways to help other people experience God's grace and compassion.

Only qualities can fill us up. So, for example, don't just empty the Sabbath of anything remotely amusing. Fill it with fun things to do that draw people closer to each other and to God. Be creative. The sky's the limit.

Don't try to restrict religious expression to one style of music. Praise God through a variety of styles that tap into a variety of emotions—joy, reverence, energy, tranquility, exuberance, reflection.

Pay more attention to eating what is set before you with a thankful heart and less to the ingredients listed on every box of cornmeal.

Appreciate people for their inner qualities, not just their outward appearance.

You want to help young ladies find security and self-esteem in Jesus Christ, not in a pair of dazzling earrings. But taking off dazzling earrings won't give anyone a sense of self-esteem in Christ.

You focus on qualities.

Healthy religion expresses something about the God we're pursuing. We have to go beyond avoidance and quantity; that burns people out. The best way to deal with the bad weeds is to cultivate the good seed. Don't just identify yourself by what you exclude. Identify yourself by what you're pursuing, the positive qualities you discover in your pursuit of God: grace and nurture, love and empathy.

Life is so much more beautiful when we have something wonderful to pursue in our lives. It ennobles everything we do.

A few shining examples

When socializing, a religion of quantity refrains from throwing wild parties, avoids drinking or carousing, and issues no invitations to the impure. Jesus suggests something different: "When you give a banquet, invite the poor, the crippled, the lame, the blind, and you will be blessed" (Luke 14:13).

The religion of quantity submits to indignities without retaliating. Jesus wants us to express something more. How about disarming the oppressive Roman soldier who forces you to carry his burden one mile by carrying it two?

The religion of quantity fasts and prays and puts on a somber spiritual face. Jesus tells us to fast and pray and put on a red dress.

He asks us to give expression to the extraordinary facts, like God's lavish forgiveness. If your million-dollar debt has been wiped out, how can you possibly hold a grudge against the guy who didn't give you the right change back?

Does God watch over us? Then give it expression. In the midst of a world hunkering down over its pursuit of financial security, be a sparrow flitting about contentedly; be a lily opened to the sun.

The New Testament is always pushing us beyond quantities to expressive qualities. There is so much in the Word waiting to be expressed and so many needs out there waiting for the touch of grace.

The religion of quantity avoids questionable amusements. The religion of qualities tries to turn them upside down.

A doctor of theology at a Paris college once invited Ignatius of Loyola to play billiards. Ignatius agreed, provided there was a stake in the game. He pointed out that he owned little beyond his own person and proposed: "If I lose, I will be your servant for a month to obey your orders. If I win, you shall do just one thing for me, and it shall be something to your advantage."

The professor willingly agreed and then lost the game of billiards. Then Loyola laid out his terms: the man must read the Spiritual Exercises, a devotional guide, and practice them for one month. As a result, the rather irreligious professor saw a marked change in his life.

When someone loses a loved one, conventional goodness prescribes that we phone our sympathy or send a condolence card. A religion of qualities finds a way to flesh-out comfort.

The terrible news about a car accident that killed several members of Madge's family came just as she, her husband, and children were preparing to move to another state. The house was in chaos. Madge had to fight through her grief to get ready—find the right clothes for the kids in all the boxes, get tickets to fly home so she could be with her mother, check on details about the funeral. As she was walking around the house in a daze, aimlessly picking things up and putting them down, the doorbell rang.

It was a neighbor. What on earth could he want?

"I've come to clean your shoes," he said simply.

Madge didn't understand. As she stared, the neighbor explained. "When my father died, it took me hours to get the children's shoes cleaned and shined for the funeral. So that's what I've come to do for you."

The neighbor settled himself on the kitchen floor and scraped and washed and shined all the shoes in the house. Watching him concentrate quietly on his task helped Madge pull her thoughts together and begin her own preparations. Later, when Madge returned from the laundry room, the neighbor was gone. But lined neatly against the wall stood all the shoes, spotless and gleaming.

When confronted by a growing crime rate, the religion of quantity locks the doors, bars the windows, and hopes for stiffer penalties. The religion of qualities checks out the streets.

In the city of Naples, bands of young orphans and outcasts, called the *scugnizzi,* lived on the streets begging, pilfering, and sometimes assisting older criminals. They were tough, wily, and apparently unreachable. But twenty-five-year-old Father Mario Borrelli wanted to try, so he became one each night after his regular duties. Dressed in the usual ragged, filthy scugnizzi get-up, he started begging at the Naples railroad terminal. The other young toughs were impressed by his style: just the right mixture of humor and pathetic humility. When a gang leader swaggered up and demanded half his take, Mario beat him up.

The incognito priest slept on basement gratings covered with old newspapers just like the others. Soon he was getting to know his new companions well as they talked around fires, heating up their scraps of food in old tin cans. And Mario discovered that all of them, even the most bitter and hardened, had a longing for home, affection, and security.

One winter evening Mario informed the gang that he'd found a place for them to stay, the little, bombed-out church of Saint Gennaro, which had been abandoned. Slowly he transformed the structure into a home and started providing the boys with nourishing meals.

One night Mario appeared in clerical robes. After his friends stopped laughing, he explained that he was, in fact, a priest. By this time the bonds he'd established were strong enough to make them stay. Mario had won their respect. And so the House of the Urchin was established, where young throwaways could find a home, hope, and the streetwise spiritual guidance of Mario Borrelli.

When unjustly accused, the religion of quantity is filled with righteous indignation. The religion of qualities tries to express something more enlightening.

There was one member of Howard Welklin's congregation who continually aimed barbs at him. He'd never experienced anything like it before in his decades of ministry—not just criticism but venomous attacks. Finally, Welklin received a letter from the man in which all the accusations were massed together in one vehement assault. The pastor had a good answer for each of the points his parishioner brought up. His criticisms were totally unjustified, and Welklin wanted very much to give it right back to the guy.

But after some serious thought and prayer, he decided on a different approach. The pastor wrote a reply back containing only four words: "Please pray for me."

Shortly afterward, the man's attitude changed radically; his animosity withered away, and he became one of the more supportive members of the congregation.

So many wonderful things can be expressed about the God Who cherishes us. There is so much room to grow in a religion of qualities.

CHAPTER FOUR

Getting Back to Love

There are many different ways in which people can be unhealthy and compulsive in their religious behavior, countless ways in which people can be legalistic. But it all revolves around one thing: a lack of love. Unhealthy religion is something you do when you can't really love. It's a substitute.

But the fact is, there's absolutely no substitute for love. That's the tragedy. You can't make up for it. You can't put anything in its place. Substitutes only make the absence of love more glaring.

I used to think that the problem of legalism would be solved as soon as people understood the concept of justification by faith clearly. When I was in college, that certainly helped me. What I'd learned about justification as I grew up in Adventist churches and schools had always been rather fuzzy. Most people seemed rather nervous about it (Yes, we're saved by faith, but . . .). I wanted to get a handle on the gospel of grace.

So I began to study the book of Romans. I looked for precise biblical definitions of terms like propitiation and redemption. I compared all the texts that tell us what we can know about our security as believers.

And at length I uncovered what was for me a compelling picture of the gospel. I had answers for all the fuzzy thinking of the past. I had a defense against legalism.

So I began to champion justification by faith before people I thought legalistic. I could argue the fine points of our redemption. I could wedge people into a corner with effective grace. I thought if they could just get this doctrine right, they'd be free.

But people weren't moved. People, in fact, could nod their heads at all my fine points and go right back to a compulsive, suffocating lifestyle.

The problem is deeper than not having the right facts. People are constrained into legalism. They just don't have the love for any other kind of religion.

I grew up in a fairly legalistic religious culture. But my parents, thank God, were nurturing, loving people. I was fortunate to grow up in a secure family environment. So I wasn't compelled to be legalistic. My heart wasn't in it. I just had some knots in my head to straighten out. And an understanding of justification by faith helped me better grasp God's grace.

But many believers struggle with insecurity all their lives. As a result, they struggle with unhealthy religion all their lives. They're not legalistic because they're stupid. They're not legalistic because they haven't quite analyzed Romans, chapter 3 correctly. They're stuck in the religion of avoidance because love hasn't given them a way out.

Love can be a hard thing to absorb. It's not enough to just nod our heads to the good news about how much God loved the whole world and gave His own Son. We can do that over and over and still put up barriers to that love. We can talk about it over and over and still remain immune to its power.

Something has to happen that makes God's love tangible; that moves us from "God loves the whole world" to "God loves me!" Something has to push us beyond the habits of the heart that keep grace out. Something has to show us that love is stronger than our most secret fears.

John is a melancholy man with cheerful eyes and wild, curly hair who grew up living a conventional Adventist life. He never went to movies, never ate a hamburger, and tried to read the Bible and pray every day.

Unfortunately, however, John never felt good enough at home. His parents were decent people, never abusive. But they gave very little affirmation. "I always felt Dad was somehow embarrassed that I was his kid," John recalls.

As a result, he never felt he was good enough, period. There was always something more he could do to please God. Maybe if he could just quit eating doughnuts, maybe if he could concentrate more when he read the Bible.

John started responding to altar calls at the age of five. And he kept doing it with great earnestness. But deep down inside he still never felt he was going to make it to heaven.

The gospel just didn't break through, John eplains. God was never really presented in church as some nit-picking ogre waiting to send people to hell. "But that was the subtext of too much Adventism I was exposed to. Not one in twenty would make it. You never knew when your name would come up at the close of probation. I lived with the idea that if your name came up and you had any unconfessed sin hanging around, you were roast beef. If you have a predisposition for insecurity, that doctrine guarantees that you will live in terror. I didn't know whether I would be able to squeak by."

John does distinctly remember one day in church when an elderly member began to talk about the wonders of God's mercy and love with great emotion. John sat there wondering what kind of strange words these were. It seemed somehow alien to his religious environment.

In college, John heard Morris Venden affirm during a week of prayer that we don't get to heaven by being good enough. At first John thought this sounded like heresy. But by the end of the week he'd been persuaded, intellectually, that we're saved by grace, not by works.

But he still couldn't go to sleep many nights because he was worrying about his sins. Had he been nice enough to people that day? Had he eaten too much dessert?

John had given up legalism in his head. But it was still there in his gut, where he lived. He couldn't quite grasp love and acceptance in his heart.

During his senior year, John fell in love with Sonya. She wasn't quite the straight-arrow Adventist he was, but they developed an intense relationship.

John sometimes accompanied her home on breaks from school, and he came to enjoy visiting with her parents very much. They were wonderful people who made him feel part of the family right away. This couple seemed to generate happiness around them. They interacted so easily with others. He hadn't experienced anything like this in his own home.

But John began to agonize about whether this girl was the right one for him. She was a great person, but were they compatible in every way? Would she be happy as his wife? With these doubts in his head, he began to wonder if he was leading her on. Finally John tormented himself into breaking up with the girl.

At the time, John was visiting at Sonya's house. He remembers the moment her Dad took him out to the patio, put his arm around his shoulder and said, "I know things aren't going too well with you and Sonya. But I want you to know that whatever happens, you're still my son."

John recalls, "That blew me away. These people liked me in a way that was connected with my core identity. I didn't have to earn my way or prove myself. They took me into their hearts out of sheer grace. I thought I knew more about theology than they would in three lifetimes. But they showed me grace. It was a huge event in my life."

John was still a very introspective, melancholy human being, however. He still had his struggles. In fact, during his first months at seminary, he was hounded by a crushing sense of guilt, imagining that he'd wronged Sonya in some way.

One night he kept beating himself up in his mind , overwhelmed by feelings of self-hatred. But then he realized: "Hey, I can't hate myself because that would be to despise Sonya's parents. I have to love the people they love."

This thought began to work its way inside John's troubled soul. It kept him from going off the edge when he felt compelled to damn himself.

And finally one night, the eyes of his heart were really opened. He'd begun to worry that the love of Sonya's parents had replaced God's love in his life. But then it hit him: "Wait a minute. That *is* God's love. That's the way He is, unconditionally loving: 'You'll always be my son.'"

That revelation stuck with him. Now he *knew* from the heart that he would always be a child of God. John says, "I became a different person. My lifestyle didn't change at all. I was still a conservative Adventist. But other people who'd known me years earlier and saw me at Andrews asked, "What's happened to you? You've changed.'

"I wasn't doing anything differently. But I'd been completely set free. A gun had been taken from my head. I wasn't changed because someone argued me into justification and grace. I was on the right side of that doctrine long before. But now I knew I was loved. I knew what God is like."

Summary of Part I

Healthy Religion—What We Pursue

Centers on seeking God
My heart says of you, "Seek his face!" Your face, Lord, I will seek (Psalm 27:8).

I am afraid that . . . your minds may somehow be led astray from your sincere and pure devotion to Christ (2 Corinthians 11:3).

Creates a devotion that fills us up
"Love the Lord your God with all your heart and with all your soul and with all your strength and with all your mind" (Luke 10:27).

Concentrates on what blesses us
Everything God created is good, and nothing is to be rejected if it is received with thanksgiving, because it is consecrated by the word of God and prayer (1 Timothy 4:4, 5).

Unhealthy Religion—What We Avoid

Centers on avoidance
Since you died with Christ to the basic principles of this world, why, as though you still belonged to it, do you submit to its rules: "Do not handle! Do not taste! Do not touch!"? . . . Such regulations indeed have an appearance of wisdom, with their self-imposed worship, their false humility and their harsh treatment of the body, but they lack any value in restraining sensual indulgence (Colossians 2:20, 21, 23).

Creates a dangerous vacuum
"When an evil spirit . . . finds the house swept clean and put in order. Then it goes and takes seven other spirits more wicked than itself, and they go in and live there. And the final condition of that man is worse than the first" (Luke 11:24-26).

Concentrates on what defiles us
They forbid people to marry and order them to abstain from certain foods, which God created to be received with thanksgiving (1 Timothy 4:3).

Healthy Religion—What We Pursue

Focuses on the good

I want you to be wise about what is good, and innocent about what is evil (Romans 16:19).

Do not be overcome by evil, but overcome evil with good (Romans 12:21).

Healthy Religion—Identity in Christ

Focuses on what God knows

Search me, O God, and know my heart; test me and know my anxious thoughts. See if there is any offensive way in me, and lead me in the way everlasting (Psalm 139:23, 24).

Surely you desire truth in the inner parts; you teach me wisdom in the inmost place (Psalm 51:6).

Majors in relationship

For to me, to live is Christ (Philippians 1:21).

Unhealthy Religion—What We Avoid

Is always reacting against the bad

The people there [in the Samaritan village] did not welcome [Jesus]. . . . When the disciples James and John saw this, they asked, "Lord, do you want us to call fire down from heaven to destroy them?" (Luke 9:53, 54).

Unhealthy Religion—Identity in Behavior

Focuses on what other people think

How can you believe if you accept praise from one another, yet make no effort to obtain the praise that comes from the only God? (John 5:44).

Many even among the leaders . . . would not confess their faith . . . for they loved praise from men more than praise from God (John 12:42, 43).

Majors in appearances

"Everything [the Pharisees] do is done for men to see: They make their phylacteries wide and the tassels on their garments long" (Matthew 23:5-7).

"When you give to the needy, do not announce it with trumpets, as the hypocrites do in the synagogues and on the streets" (Matthew 6:2).

Gets identity from whom it knows

I consider everything a loss compared to the surpassing greatness of knowing Christ Jesus my Lord (Philippians 3:8).

Gains a secure position

God raised us up with Christ and seated us with him in the heavenly realms in Christ Jesus (Ephesians 2:6).

Healthy Religion—Qualities

Nurtures qualities

The kingdom of God is not a matter of eating and drinking, but of righteousness, peace and joy in the Holy Spirit, because anyone who serves Christ in this way is pleasing to God and approved by men (Romans 14:17, 18).

Therefore, as God's chosen people, holy and dearly loved, clothe yourselves with compassion, kindness, humility, gentleness and patience. . . . And over all these virtues put on love, which binds them all together in perfect unity (Colossians 3:12, 14).

Gets identity from what it's not

The Pharisee stood up and prayed about himself: "God, I thank you that I am not like other men—robbers, evildoers, adulterers—or even like this tax collector" (Luke 18:11, 12).

Always struggles for position

"Beware of the teachers of the law. They like to walk around in flowing robes and love to be greeted in the marketplaces and have the most important seats in the synagogues and the places of honor at banquets" (Luke 20:46).

Unhealthy Religion—Quantities

Hopes in quantity

"The multitude of your sacrifices—what are they to me?" says the Lord. "I have more than enough of burnt offerings, of rams and the fat of fattened animals" (Isaiah 1:11).

"When you pray, do not keep on babbling like pagans, for they think they will be heard because of their many words" (Matthew 6:7).

Healthy Religion—Qualities	**Unhealthy Religion—Quantities**

Results in transformation

Neither circumcision nor uncircumcision means anything; what counts is a new creation (Galatians 6:15).

Simulates holiness

"You give a tenth of your spices—mint, dill and cumin. But you have neglected the more important matters of the law—justice, mercy and faithfulness" (Matthew 23:23).

"You clean the outside of the cup and dish, but inside they are full of greed and self-indulgence" (Matthew 23:25).

Expands life immeasurably

In Christ all the fullness of the Deity lives in bodily form, and you have been given fullness in Christ (Colossians 2:9, 10).

His divine power has given us everything we need for life and godliness through our knowledge of [Jesus] (2 Peter 1:3).

Constricts life

The Jews said to the man who had been healed, "It is the Sabbath; the law forbids you to carry your mat" (John 5:10).

"And you experts in the law, woe to you, because you load people down with burdens they can hardly carry, and you yourselves will not lift one finger to help them" (Luke 11:46).

Expresses something great about God

Whether you eat or drink or whatever you do, do it all for the glory of God (1 Corinthians 10:31).

Sinks into pettiness

How is it that you are turning back to those weak and miserable principles? Do you wish to be enslaved by them all over again? You are observing special days and months and seasons and years! I fear for you, that somehow I have wasted my efforts on you (Galatians 4:9-11).

The Truth:
Me Versus Error

CHAPTER FIVE

Do You Have to Be Right?

For many Adventists, Jim represented the last great stand for truth in our time. Donations poured into his ministry. People who thought too many Adventist ministers were compromising the "straight testimony" saw Jim as a champion, uncorrupted by the errors that had seeped into the church.

Jim wasn't afraid to say what was wrong with the Catholics. He wasn't afraid to say what was wrong with the Methodists or Baptists or Lutherans. When the *It Is Written* telecast tried a different approach with George Vandeman's series, "What I Like About . . . ," which looked at the biblical truths Luther, Wesley, and others had recovered, Jim thundered, "You might as well preach 'What I Like About the Whore of Babylon.' "

Jim knew how to draw lines between truth and error. And he came to believe that only he was drawing the right lines. All the mainstream Adventist ministries, in his view, were in bed with apostate religion.

Jim liked to preach beside a stack of Ellen White books. And he quoted her at length, "giving it to them hard," as he said, about slipping standards and imminent persecution.

At one point he decided to take on the celebration services that were springing up in some Adventist churches. He pointed out just what a terrible threat this contemporary style of worship posed to bedrock Adventist beliefs. Hundreds of thousands of dollars poured into his ministry as a result.

Jim produced a video supposedly exposing the grievous errors of another Adventist evangelist. Careful editing of the evangelist's messages on videotape made him appear to make controversial statements. He also began a personal crusade against Martin Weber, the author of *Adventist Hot Potatoes*.

Jim always managed to find some scandalous error to spotlight. His newsletter could be counted on to sensationalize some problem in the church or in the General Conference.

Jim apparently had a tremendous talent for exposing error. He knew exactly why everybody else was wrong, but couldn't seem to see his own problems.

Others, however, reported that he was addicted to pornography, that he felt compelled to be the center of attention at all times, that he'd driven away many staff members with abusive tirades.

They said he could persuade a whole church from the pulpit to fast and pray for a coming crusade and then go home to a huge Sabbath dinner, topped off by a "chocolate bonanza."

Jim just couldn't seem to get a handle on these "minor problems." But he knew exactly why contemporary Christian music is the scourge of the earth.

Jim's colleagues realized, at length, that this man had a tremendous need to be somebody, maybe a *pathological* need to be somebody.

Jim had become somebody by being right, by showing how everybody else was wrong. That's the place he carved out for himself.

But what is most disturbing about the sorry tale of Jim and his ministry is how powerfully he appealed to many Adventists. Something about the lines he kept drawing appealed to them. Something about the us-versus-them perspective inspired them. There was something about "being right" in this way that struck a chord with many loyal church members. They felt intense loyalty toward a man who seemed to wield "the truth" in such a decisive manner.

Why? Why did so many follow a man with such negative ministry?

I believe part of the reason lies in why people join the church and why they remain in the church. I am afraid that many people may become Seventh-day Adventists for the wrong reasons. It's possible to do the right thing for very unhealthy reasons.

Seventh-day Adventism is a very distinctive Protestant denomination. It's not just another church. It has seen itself as a reform movement, calling people out of the "apostate daughters of Babylon" and into the remnant.

Adventists point to truths that almost everyone else seems to be ignoring.

Everybody else goes to church on Sunday.

Everybody else believes in the immortal soul.

Everybody else believes the law has been done away with.

It may well be true that Adventists have got it right in a lot of areas where other Christians have got it wrong. But we need to be aware of how this affects us and how it affects people who are joining the church.

Being right when everybody else is wrong has great appeal to certain kinds of people. Some individuals have a desperate need to be right—and try to meet that need in the wrong way. Usually it's because they never received the affirmation that made them feel right as human beings. And they never learned how to give and receive love in a healthy way. So they are continually frustrated.

People who can't be loved have to be right—that's the bottom line. But they can't be right, or good, in a healthy way. They can only be right in the sense of being correct. They've got to have the real facts, the inside information.

And the only way they can prove this is by being more right, more correct, than their neighbors. That's why they are obsessed with hunting down errors. That's why they emphasize having the truth so much. That's why what matters to them in the end time is having the correct theology, avoiding deception and error.

Imagine what happens when a person like this finds out about a denomination that has many unique truths. Bingo. He joins up. Suddenly he's got a whole new arsenal with which to prove himself right and everyone else wrong.

Please remember; this doesn't mean that the doctrines of a distinctive church are wrong. It simply means they can be used in the wrong way.

I became acquainted with a Scandinavian gentleman, who had been baptized into the Adventist Church, one day after a sermon on the remnant. He decided that this was the church he wanted to give his allegiance to.

Gunter is a hard-working man, an independent thinker who works with his hands but likes to read widely. And he is very sure that Adventists have got all the doctrines right. He is good at arguing the right positions. And he can't understand why anyone would ever leave the true church.

But he doesn't understand his wife at all. He doesn't understand why his marriage is withering away. Gunter is in touch with all the right facts, but he's completely out of touch with people's feelings. He pours his spare time into building a huge speedboat instead of listening to the agonized spiritual conflict that his wife can only share with others.

Gunter's life is falling apart. But he belongs to the right organization. That's his consolation. He's not so good with relationships, but he's great with information.

On the surface it may seem that people who have to be right make good Adventists. They devour all the doctrines; they appear to be spiritually hungry. But too often all this is just about ammunition, not a relationship with God. After they've signed on to the 27 Fundamental Beliefs, they can go back to Uncle Harry and tell him why his Baptist theology is all wet. They can visit Aunt Margaret and prove to her—really prove to her—that her beloved Catholic church is a lair for the antichrist.

This has little to do with sharing love or grace. It has more to do with proving yourself right by proving someone else wrong. For example, some people can talk endlessly about the chosen, the remnant precisely because they don't feel chosen and never will feel chosen without God's supernatural intervention.

The more some individuals can prove that others are in error, the more secure they can feel. It's not a very good security, of course. There's always that gnawing lack of love inside. There's always something driving them on. And so they become addicted to argument. Insecure people can argue about everything. Winning arguments is their substitute for winning love.

We have, unfortunately, a lot of Adventists who like to argue. We seem to attract many people who like to argue. That can produce unhealthy religion.

Let's take a look at some of the things that can happen when people fall into the religion of having to be right. These all relate to our relationship with "the truth." Sometimes the way we use "the truth" actually gets in the way of the real Truth sinking into our hearts.

Facts replace feelings

The Adventist Church began as a reform movement. And one of the things our earnest young pioneers wanted to reform was doctrine. They were so indignant about the spiritual impotence and doctrinal sloppiness of the churches around them that they decided to rediscover Christian belief from the ground up. They would start all over again. They would discard every religious assumption. They would study the Word of God exhaustively. Every belief would be tested in the light of the explicit statements of Scripture.

Generally, they ended up testing truths by proof-text. They strung together a series of verses that logically progressed from one point to another until a clear conclusion could be proven. The sum of these texts was a doctrine. Sometimes those verses followed a very circuitous route in and out of one Bible book after another. But those journeys through Scripture always began from a very keen devotion to the truth of God's Word. And generations of Adventists have been marking their Bibles and following in the footsteps of the pioneers.

Adventists have always cared deeply about biblical truth. In fact, when someone joins the church, he or she is said to have "come into the truth." Our Bible studies take people through our "27 Fundamental Beliefs." We proclaim "Truth for the End Time." We champion "Present Truth."

Adventists have always emphasized Christian education. Our schools are the envy of many larger Protestant denominations. We are good at developing the mind.

As Adventists we've always prided ourselves on our doctrinal integrity. That's our strength. Doctrinal integrity is a good thing. Caring about exactly what Scripture says is a good thing.

But every strength has its pitfalls. Any strength can turn into a weakness. A church that concentrates on finding "the truth" can become an exclusively left-brained denomination.

Adventists are into concepts, not feelings. When we talk about feelings, we usually talk about their perils. Feelings are not to be trusted. Feelings lead us astray. Feelings can be manipulated by the enemy. We're supposed to make decisions based on facts, not feelings.

We also warn people about relying on mere "experiences." We are suspicious of the Holy Spirit doing this or that in someone's life—especially someone in another denomination. We get nervous about a Holy Spirit Who might act dramatically. What happens to you isn't "the truth." Only the Word of God is "the Truth." You have to rely on the clear statements of Scripture.

All this is good advice, of course—to a certain extent. We have to base our beliefs as Christians on the revelation in the Bible. It's true that God's Word is more reliable than experiences or feelings. But what we forget is that God's Word is also more reliable than our intellects. Our heads aren't infallible; they can be manipulated just as our hearts can be.

It's easy to point the finger at believers who are too emotional, those soft-headed people who just gush about Jesus and who don't have a firm grasp of Scripture. It escapes us that we can be too hard-headed. We may have a firm grasp of Scripture and yet never let God touch our emotions, never touch Him with ours.

Traditional Adventist worship is not an emotional experience. Prying an "amen" out of most white congregations is like getting a duck to bark. Part of the reason we malign charismatics so much is that their exuberance seems so alien.

But healthy religion involves all of us—body, mind, heart, and soul. Healthy religion involves our emotions. Adventists are, of course, quite used to giving lip service to the idea of wholeness, of human beings as multidimensional creatures. We advertise that perspective in our schools and hospitals. But that's just an abstract concept. That's not the same as really dealing with our feelings.

God wants to get inside our hearts as well as straighten out our heads. We've worked long and hard at doctrinal integrity. And that effort is to be commended. But I don't think we've even touched the surface of emotional integrity. And that's because we have allowed facts to replace feelings for so long.

I see it happen over and over. People who are emotionally crippled major in the right facts. They become experts at dispensing the right facts. People who are wrestling with feelings of insecurity, anger, and fear keep all those unruly emotions stuffed out of sight with their correct knowledge. The right facts become a substitute for good feelings.

A good friend of mine has become a champion of justification by faith against the legalists and perfectionists in the church. Larry has good reason to concentrate on grace. It is his defense against the horrendous childhood he endured under the religious tyranny of his father. The concept of unmerited favor helps him fend off the dark shadow of an endlessly demanding God—a distortion of his heavenly Father that his earthly father created.

Although my friend has made tremendous strides to leave his dysfunctional background behind him, he still wrestles with ugly feelings; he's still haunted by the past. Deep down in his heart there's pain, anger, bitterness, and a longing for what might have been.

Sometimes I sense in Larry's passionate defense of justification by faith an unresolved battle with his father. He's still fighting off the cruel put-downs, the sneers, and the simple pig-headedness of that man. He's trying to argue him out of all that. His confrontations with right-wing Adventists are really confrontations with the man he could never stand up to as a child.

Larry wields the facts. And he has the right ones, praise God. He has a hold on the gospel and has learned to express tolerance even in the midst of theological battle. But I sometimes wish he could feel God's grace more deeply, that it could seep into his soul. I wish he still didn't have to carry such a burden. I wish he could defend himself with more than just these good facts.

Others I've met wield "the truth" as a defense in a much more dogmatic way than Larry. As a scriptwriter for Adventist telecasts, I have the privilege of interacting with some of the brightest minds in the church. Occasionally I've been part of prolonged theological discussions—confidential ones where people can frankly share their views on all kinds of topics. We've debated predestination, the omniscience of God, the inspiration of Scripture.

I've noticed that many of us tend to settle on a certain doctrinal point of view and then build a little fortress around it—with relevant texts, of course. The discussions have been very stimulating. Our minds sharpen one another. But sometimes I sense a great sadness underneath it all.

I get the feeling that our heated debates are driven by much more than just the pursuit of truth. There are unexpressed emotions, feelings of inadequacy, and anger bubbling under the surface. That's why we can go on debating some minor detail about Christ's position in the heavenly sanctuary so passionately. It's the painful emotions that drive people on. But we don't deal with them. We just keep playing with the facts. We try to use our great competence with the truth to hide our incompetence with deep emotions. We use the right facts to make up for the wrong feelings.

The strength of the Adventist Church, its doctrinal integrity, can become ideal cover for individuals who can't relate to God on an emotional level. Such people can devote themselves to learning all the right doctrines, to processing all this good information. And they can go on refining their views on law and grace, on the Sabbath, on the mark of the beast, their entire Christian lives.

Remember, just because doctrine can be used in the wrong way, that doesn't make doctrine wrong. It just means that something good can be abused—a strength can turn into a weakness.

But we do have to deal with a chronic problem: trying to use facts to replace feelings, trying to use a whole lot of the right knowledge to replace a whole lot of emptiness inside. Knowledge can be used as a substitute for love. Doctrine can be used as a substitute for love.

Pointing out error

The religion of legalism puts *sin*—the avoidance of sin—at the center of the Christian life. The religion of having to be right puts *error* at the center of the Christian life. Spirituality is reduced to a matter of rooting out error. Believers assume we must always remain vigilant against the error that may creep in and corrupt our righteous souls. We must always guard against Satan's efforts to deceive us in countless ways. We must expose the distortions of truth that spring up when we least expect them.

A religion centered around having to be right never tires of repeating this principle: Satan mixes in a little error with the truth in order to deceive the faithful. People assert this because, after all, the enemy masquerades as an angel of light in order to make his insidious heresies more attractive. So we must take care to examine every religious message that comes our way for possible mistakes.

There is some truth in this principle, of course. Satan does try to deceive the elect. He's not lacking in tricks up his sleeve.

But something very unhealthy happens when this becomes our primary perspective, when we look at all of life from this point of view: *beware of error.*

I see Adventists doing this frequently. We evaluate some "outside" speaker or author and find a flaw in the message, something that isn't quite in synch with good Adventist theology. And we immediately proceed to warn our neighbors about the dangers of this "error." All the good stuff presented is just a coverup to get this false teaching into our midst.

When I was a student missionary working at the SDA English schools in Japan, I very much enjoyed one of the speakers who came to our teacher's retreat. He had a unique way of making theological principles easy to grasp.

So later, when I found a couple of sermons on audio tape by this same pastor, I eagerly snatched them up. They were recordings of a series on the essentials of spiritual growth he'd given to a group of college students.

At one point in his presentation, the man paused to make some comments on the charismatic movement. A couple of revivals had broken out on Adventist college campuses, and he wanted to make sure his audience understood the difference between our revivals and the things that were happening in charismatic renewal.

What struck me from the beginning was his assumption that the devil lay behind the whole thing. He didn't say this explicitly, but it was obvious that's what he believed. He began to explain in detail why the charismatic movement was so deceptive.

The pastor had evidently encountered a few charismatics who were on fire for Jesus, people who'd made quite an impression. But after describing their bright-eyed devotion, he asserted this: you can talk about Jesus, you can be enthusiastic about Jesus, but that doesn't mean you have the truth.

Well, I could understand that. Paying lip service to Christ doesn't guarantee that you have a real relationship with Him.

Next, the pastor stated that he'd observed manifestations of what appeared to be fruits of the Spirit among these people. They were loving, they were joyous, they had peace. But, he cautioned, false revival can generate qualities that appear very spiritual. People may appear to be transformed, but the devil can still hide the truth from them.

Now I began to feel uneasy. If love and joy and peace don't count, what does? Does the devil go around transforming individuals and making them more Christlike so he can slip in some imperfect theology in among the unsuspecting?

In conclusion, the pastor admitted that these charismatic acquaintances of his had gone so far as to manifest a profound thirst for the Word—they were always studying the Bible.

Even this, however, didn't faze the speaker. It only demonstrated how profoundly subtle the devil could be in creating a counterfeit movement. It only showed him that even people immersing themselves in Scripture weren't necessarily a sign that genuine spiritual renewal was taking place.

At this point I came unglued. What did this man want? What hope is there for any of us? Devotion to Christ wasn't enough. People transformed, people exhibiting spiritual qualities wasn't enough. That was somehow an illusion. Even dedication to the study of the Word wasn't enough.

After turning off my tape recorder, I realized that it didn't really matter what these charismatic acquaintances of the speaker demonstrated. They were in error by definition. Angels bouncing off the walls as they spoke, people rising from the dead around them—nothing would have made any difference. It would all have been chalked up to "counterfeit signs."

These people didn't have the "27 Fundamental Beliefs." So they weren't really in the game. Their revival wasn't even in the ballpark. It had to be a counterfeit.

It was impossible for this man to believe than any group that did not observe the seventh-day Sabbath could generate the real thing: spiritual revival. These charismatics were obviously mixed up about that, as well as about a few other doctrinal matters. And so everything else good about their movement was simply an elaborate disguise to make error more attractive.

After listening to evaluations like this, I can't help thinking of the people who constantly "evaluated" Christ during His ministry. The Pharisees had decided *a priori* that Jesus couldn't possibly be the Messiah. He simply didn't fit in with their theology or their religious culture. He didn't have their stamp of approval—and He was going about preaching to multitudes anyway. So they had to explain away all the wonderful things He was doing. They had to explain lepers who were no longer lepers, prostitutes who were no longer prostitutes, and even dead people who were no longer dead. They gave it their best shot.

They questioned his parentage and his town of origin. They accused Him of breaking the law and defiling the temple. And once they even claimed that He was casting out demons by the power of Beelzebub, the devil himself. In other words, the devil was allowing Jesus to free people from bondage to himself, from a life of degradation, so that such miracles would fool people, so that this false Messiah would trap the unwary.

Jesus pointed out how ludicrous it would be for the devil to fight against himself. The truth was, the evil one had to be bound and gagged in order for his captives to go free.

This is a truth that ought to inform our religious criticism. It ought to give us pause. With our attitude that an "outside" speaker or movement—despite all the good that results—can't possibly be Spirit-led, we come dangerously close to the derangement of the Pharisees.

One of the big problems with this perspective of one-flaw-contaminates-the-whole is that we only apply it to other people. That's the only way it seems to make sense. We only use it to evaluate outsiders, never ourselves.

But if we did apply it to ourselves, our own church, our own lives, then we'd all be doomed. Nobody would be in the ballpark. You couldn't listen to anyone. Everybody would be the devil disguised as an angel of light.

Why? Because nobody is perfect. Nobody's heart is perfect. Nobody's head is perfect. No human being on the planet ever speaks the truth perfectly. Nobody mirrors God's perspective with 100 percent accuracy. We *all* have a little bit of error mixed in with our truth.

Individuals who are compelled to stand in judgment can never really grasp this fact. Their unexamined assumption is that the place where they stand is some kind of uncontaminated lookout point from which they can infallibly rule on what is truth and what is error.

But, of course, the more time we spend trying to take the speck out of some brother's eye, trying to dissect the error buried in some otherwise inspiring message, the more likely we are to carry around an unseen log in our own eye.

Adventists have long believed that we possess an extremely convenient test for dividing the sheep from the goats: the seventh-day Sabbath. Looking at our own experience, looking at how we accepted "the truth," we naturally assume that if any believer is at all open to the leading of God, he or she will become convicted about the right day of worship. If they are in the Word and still going to church on Sunday, then they must be resisting the enlightening Spirit of God in some way.

Well, this game works both ways, folks. People on the outside could look at many of our congregations and conclude this: Any believer at all open to the leading of God's will should at least understand grace. If they are in the Word and still struggling with legalism, then they must be resisting the Spirit in some way.

Does anyone doubt that many of our members are still struggling with legalism, that it continues to haunt our churches? At least we're able to admit the problem now. We're able to see what it's done to our kids. We're beginning to understand how it stifles joyous worship in our churches.

From our perspective inside the church, we simply say, "This is a problem we're working on; nobody's perfect." But why shouldn't someone on the outside conclude that this bit of error has contaminated the whole? Why shouldn't someone conclude that Adventism is a counterfeit movement? Sure, they have a wonderful health message. Sure, they've clarified the prophecies of Revelation. Sure, they have a wonderful picture of the great controversy. Sure, they are faithful, tithe-paying, church-going, commandment-keeping believers. But all that good stuff is simply a coverup for this bit of error, this legalism that contaminates the whole. All the great things about Adventists simply show how subtle Satan can be when he creates a deception.

It doesn't feel so good when people apply this principle to us, does it? It feels outrageously unfair, in fact.

Many Adventists have subconsciously assumed that having the right package of truth, having those "27 Fundamental Beliefs," guarantees that all spiritual light on the planet has to originate from our group. We're the right church because we have the right doctrines.

And so we expect someone to join, say, the Seventh-day Adventist Church of Centerville, USA, because of that package of correct concepts. And if there's a lot of gossip and backbiting in the Centerville church, well that's just human nature; nobody's perfect.

But what if behavior is part of the truth we're presenting? What if the quality of our fellowship is part of the message we're giving? What if the identity of a church is tied to more than the list of abstractions to which it pledges allegiance?

In that case, a church like Centerville's would be, heaven forbid, full of "error." That spirit of criticism and quarrelsomeness would contaminate its biblical teaching. And a new believer coming into this fellowship might well see his or her faith crumble.

Any claim that we "have the truth" should make any sane Christian tremble. Having the twenty-seven fundamentals is just the beginning. That's just the framework. What about the *spirit* of a particular church, what about the *qualities* it projects? What kind of truth is being presented by *relationships* within the congregation?

All this should make us very cautious about judging other churches, other movements. We're all vulnerable here. We all live in glass houses, and too many of us think we're "discerning error" when we're just throwing rocks.

On one of my periodic Christmas visits to Houston to see my relatives, I was happily surprised to find that my cousin Lisa had found her way to Christ. This budding Houston socialite had never shown any interest in religion before. But now I saw her glowing because of a new "relationship with Jesus." And I discovered that Lisa's conversion had come about through charismatic believers.

She seemed almost giddy as she recounted how exciting her spiritual journey had become. We were sitting on the carpet of her mother's formal living room, a place of exquisite furnishings that I remember rarely entering as a kid. I couldn't help wondering if her conversion was as fragile as the Chinese painted panels or the finely carved coffee table.

So I asked her a lot of questions. I'd heard that charismatics are big on emotion, big on phenomena. Was this just an emotional encounter with some not-so-holy-spirit?

Lisa talked about Jesus, she talked about her discoveries, she talked about the quality of her friendships with other believers. I saw real spiritual life blossoming in front of me. And above all, Lisa talked about how much she was enjoying the Bible; she just couldn't get enough of it.

Well, despite my prejudices about anything to do with charismatics, I had to praise God for this girl's new faith. What had happened to her was good. I wasn't going to pretend that her getting into the Word was some elaborate scheme to leave her as deceived as she'd been before. I wasn't going to twist all these blessings into some kind of counterfeit.

Good is good, even if it happens in another church. The spirit of love and joy is a good thing, period, even if it happens in a group we think is pretty weird. People getting into the Word is a good thing, period.

It's perverse to try to turn the fruits of the Spirit into the deeds of the enemy. It borders on blasphemy. The log in our eye can become big indeed.

Unhealthy religion always puts up a filter between ourselves and reality. We almost never look at things as they are. We see them only according to how they fit into categories. That can't be a sincere believer over there, she's got a dove pin on; must be a charismatic. That person poring over an open Bible can't really be taking in God's truth, he's wearing a cross; must be Catholic, and we all know Catholics never get into the Word. Those thousands of people coming forward in that stadium with tears streaming down their faces can't really be coming to Christ; the evangelist up on the platform issuing the call doesn't believe in the Sabbath; he can't be acting on Christ's behalf.

On several occasions I've listened to Adventists pose what they believe to be a profound moral dilemma: would you go to a Pentecostal service if you knew you could be healed of some chronic malady? This is a dilemma, because they assume the devil is the one performing the healings there. In other words, is getting cured of cancer worth letting Satan into your life?

Why do we make such dark assumptions about other churches? Why are we so incredibly hard on other believers? I think we give even hardened atheists a little more credit than this.

If I go into a service and someone is asking Jesus to heal someone, I don't assume this is the devil's playground. If someone is praying with apparent sincerity in Jesus' name, then I am going to praise God if anybody gets up from a wheelchair.

I may not like the healer's flashy maroon suit. I may not like his slick hairdo. I may not like the shouting in the service or the pumping organ or the sweating matrons speaking in tongues. But I don't think I have the right to attribute all this to Satan just because it wars against my tastes.

Once James and John tried to prevent a nondisciple from trying to cast out a demon in Jesus' name. After all, he was "not one of us."

Jesus replied, "Do not stop him. No one who does a miracle in my name can in the next moment say anything bad about me, for whoever is not against us is for us" (Mark 9:39, 40).

Jesus didn't occupy himself trying to find flaws in this outsider, this amateur exorcist. He affirmed instead that anyone who even gives a cup of water to a needy individual in Christ's name would "certainly not lose his reward."

James and John were just acting out of human nature. It's so easy to spot the "error" in other groups yet so difficult to detect it in our own. Charismatics are an easy target, for example, because they occupy the opposite end of the religious spectrum from traditional Adventism. It's not difficult for us to point out their weaknesses.

They are grounded in miraculous phenomena more than they are grounded in Scripture.

They are guided by their emotions more than by principle.

They make everybody try to speak in tongues as a sign of being filled with the Spirit.

We can see all this a mile away. What we can't see is that our complaints about "all this emotionalism" come from hearts that seem incapable of exuberant worship.

What we can't see is that we are instinctively suspicious of *all* phenomena that might manifest an unbounded Spirit.

What we can't see is that we explain away what the New Testament calls "ecstatic utterance"—tongues—as a condensed course in foreign languages.

Instead of pulling out our tweezers for the other guy all the time, it's far better to feel around for that log in our own eye. If charismatics raise their hands too much, we sit on them too much. If they are too loud in their praises, we are too dumb. If they are too emotional, we are too dry.

Extremes always justify themselves by pointing to the opposite extreme: We don't want to go there; we must avoid that "error." So we keep reacting against those "unbalanced people," that contrasting style of spirituality, and become more and more unbalanced ourselves in the other direction.

It's sad when churches become identified by what they *exclude*. When all the focus is on keeping unwanted elements *out*, pretty soon you find there isn't that much left inside. And this isn't just a problem of prejudice against certain worship styles or types of people or religious groups. It applies to ideas as well, to truth. Sometimes we believers, in our efforts to hold on tightly to the pure message, to keep it from being contaminated, find that it slips through our fingers.

You've probably heard it said of some very stubborn person: "It would take major surgery to get a new idea into his head." Unfortunately, that's sometimes true of churches. We can get to the point where all our windows are boarded up—to keep error out—but very little light gets in.

It's very dangerous to cut yourself off from everything outside your group.

I remember a dear friend of the family in the Illinois church I attended as a college student. She didn't want to read any periodical or book that didn't come from an Adventist publishing house. She didn't want to listen to any preacher who didn't have Adventist credentials. Some days she hardly wanted to read anything not penned by Ellen White. After all, God had given this woman all the truth we needed for our time.

It's understandable, of course, to get your principle spiritual diet from the church where you have found the truth. But it's not healthy to restrict your diet exclusively to one source.

People need outside input. Dysfunctional families always isolate their members. Everyone has to process reality in a certain way; the flow of information in and out is tightly controlled. Churches can become dysfunctional too. Ingrown churches—churches that cut themselves off from outside input—become sick. They become cultic.

The Branch Davidian group is a classic example. In that tightly knit group of earnest believers, only David Koresh had the truth; he alone could interpret reality for his followers. And once he got a monopoly on the truth, Koresh couldn't resist the temptation to exploit it.

He had the right to marry other people's wives. He had the right to arm his followers for the end times.

Why did these people, many of whom came from Adventist backgrounds, follow this lunatic to such an extent? How could they give their lives for him? Because nobody else could get through. Nobody else could tell them what a huge mistake they were making. Everybody else was "in error." Everybody else was captured by the antichrist. Everybody else was out to get them. Only Koresh knew what was really happening in the world.

A religion of having to be right invariably becomes a religion of having to make everybody else wrong.

CHAPTER SIX

Can You Tell What's Most Important?

Much of the teaching of Jesus that has been preserved for us was actually first given in the heat of battle. During His ministry on earth, He had to carry out almost daily maneuvers against the plots and complaints and accusations of His religious rivals. The Pharisees represent the epitome of left-brained, anal-retentive, obsessive, facts-replace-feelings, religion. They were world-class legalists. They ran the Olympics of hypocrisy, and their competitive religious games went on all the time.

If you look at Christ's encounters with these individuals, you will notice that they often revolved around perspective. They were a long battle over perspective and values: What's important? What's not so important?

Healing a blind man was important. The fact that Jesus chose to mix a little mud to put over the man's eyes in order to do it, the fact that this happened on the Sabbath, was not so important. The Pharisees didn't get this.

Healing a man who'd been paralyzed for thirty-eight years was important. The fact that he subsequently carried his mat around on the Sabbath was not. The Pharisees didn't get this.

Healing people deformed by leprosy was important. The fact that you might become ceremonially unclean while doing so was not. The Pharisees didn't get this.

The loving gesture of a repentant prostitute who washed Jesus' feet was important. The fact that she didn't observe social decor at a party was not. The Pharisees didn't get this.

The widow's mite was important. Making a show of your big contribution to the temple was not so important. The Pharisees didn't get this.

The Pharisees didn't get a lot of things. They got lost in their religious facts. They got lost in being experts. They lost touch with feelings of compassion and humanity. They always had a response to some problem from their codified tradition; they never had a response from the heart.

The Pharisees lost perspective. Unhealthy, have-to-be-right religion does that. People get so preoccupied with being correct in the details that they can no longer distinguish the trivial from the momentous. Everything has to go into a category. Everything has to be either black or white. People lose the capacity to make subtle judgments. They can't distinguish between a man working on the Sabbath and a healed paralytic carrying his mat joyfully toward the temple on the Sabbath. They can't distinguish between the improper advances of a prostitute and the touch of a fallen woman reaching out in faith. They can't distinguish between a show of generosity and generosity of the heart.

Unhealthy religion is unbalanced. It lacks perspective. It invests enormous energy in correctly tithing "mint, dill and cumin," and neglects "justice, mercy, and faithfulness." It majors in details and minors in things of the heart.

It's remarkable how much religious meaning people can invest in the accessories of the Christian life. You would think, for example, that where you happen to find the song lyrics during a Sabbath worship service would be of no great consequence. Wrong.

Whether you find them in a book, a hymnal, or projected up on a screen seems portentous for some individuals; it carries moral weight. Looking up at the words on a screen, it is solemnly affirmed, opens to the door to a frivolous kind of worship. Without that solid hymnbook to hold, your hands are left free, and some in the congregation may just raise them in some unguarded moment. People complain that as we sing these contemporary gospel refrains over and over we're becoming just like all the other churches. We should be distinctive. (As if we haven't been just like all the other churches for 100 years when we were singing all those nineteenth century hymns.)

It's fine for people to prefer one style of music over another in worship. It's fine to have tastes. But it's unhealthy to deify those tastes, to make your likes moral and your dislikes immoral.

Unhealthy, compulsive people have a hard time distinguishing between what is central to the faith and what is marginal. They lack perspective. They are working so hard to prove they are right or to defend their turf or to be on the inside that they turn minor differences into battlegrounds. This has happened throughout the history of the Christian church.

Majoring in the details

The New Testament has a great deal to say about how wonderful Christ is. Jesus is the Lord of glory, King of kings, magnificent above all else. But churches, in trying to reflect that glory, have taken detours into elaborate liturgies and traditions. The precise way in which Christ is praised has been turned into a doctrine. Denominations have wrangled over the right way to worship for centuries.

During the reign of Czar Alexis, the Russian church stood on the edge of revival and reformation. Groups of missionaries traveled through Mother Russia calling clergy and lay people back to sincere spiritual devotion. But then, tragically, the movement broke up.

Leaders began disputing over correct forms of worship. The official church insisted that the sign of the cross be made with three fingers raised instead of two. They decreed that the threefold Alleluia, not the twofold, be sung in worship. Thousands of people, called "old ritualists," believed that such liturgical changes signaled the end of the world. Many sacrificed their lives in opposition.

When Christ presided over His last supper and instituted what has become known as the Communion service, He repeated these simple words, "Do this in remembrance of Me." He wanted His followers, in taking the bread as His broken body and the drink as His shed blood, to remember His sacrifice on the cross.

But churches couldn't leave it at that. People with great intellects constructed elaborate doctrines around this sacrament. They went to great pains to create theologies of the bread and wine. And, incredibly enough, people who call themselves Christians have even been willing to torture and burn other believers for having a different perspective on this issue!

Here's a remarkable interrogation from an ecclesiastical courtroom in sixteenth-century London. Bishop Bonner is quizzing a young man named Thomas Haukes, who stands condemned as a heretic.

"Do you not believe," the bishop asks indignantly, "that there remaineth in the blessed sacrament of the altar . . . the very body and blood of Christ?"

Haukes answers simply, "I do believe as Christ hath taught me."

This doesn't satisfy Bonner. He wants to know exactly what his prisoner thinks Christ meant by the words, "Take, eat; this is My body."

Haukes admits he doesn't agree with the current church doctrine, called transubstantiation, affirming that the bread and wine actually become the literal body and blood of Jesus. He points out that none of the apostles had ever taught it.

This further angers the bishop. "Ah, sir! You will have no more than the Scripture teacheth?"

That is precisely Thomas Hauke's position. He wants to be taught from the Word of God. Instead he is burned at the stake.

People turn minor details into major doctrinal battlefields. As a result, they go off into all kinds of religious tangents—often with tragic consequences.

In the Adventist Church we have a special challenge in this area. We possess what we call "distinctive truths," beliefs that set us apart from other Christians.

In truth, most traditional denominations have distinctive beliefs; some relate to church liturgy or governance, some relate to theological categories like justification and sanctification, a few relate to details like being baptized in Jesus' name only, having no musical instruments in worship, or believing that Britain is the new Israel.

When a church has a distinctive truth, it naturally wants to emphasize that truth. Why talk about what everyone else is talking about?

Adventists believe we have been given special end-time truths for the world. This sense of uniqueness makes our proselytizing especially urgent. Our package of distinctive beliefs, sometimes called the five pillars of Adventism, includes: the Sabbath, the Second Coming, the sanctuary, the state of the dead, and spiritual gifts (a euphemism for the ministry of Ellen White).

But as it turns out, quite a few other churches share some of these beliefs. The Advent movement of the late nineteenth century was even more successful than most Adventists realize. Many churches that virtually ignored the Second Coming before now boldly proclaim it, although some in the form of a secret rapture.

We are also not alone in our affirmation of the unconscious state of the dead who will be awakened by the Second Coming. And there are even a few other denominations that affirm the seventh-day Sabbath.

So, when we look around for the one doctrine that is most distinctive in the midst of our distinctive beliefs, we end up with the sanctuary doctrine, the investigative judgment.

That is the only specific doctrine discovered by Seventh-day Adventists that no other major denomination in the world affirms. And so naturally, Adventists have paid a lot of attention to this belief. We've written many books about it. We've interpreted it in various ways. We've argued about it at great length. Many pastors have had to leave the church because they could no longer believe it.

The feeling is: This is something unique we have to share with the world. No one else is talking about it. So it must be important.

I don't want to argue the finer points of the investigative judgment in this book. My burden is to point out an assumption connected with the doctrine: because it's very unique, it's most important.

I believe this is a very dangerous assumption for religious people to make. It's at the root of a great deal of confusion and heartache.

Admittedly, there's a certain logic to the assumption. We believe God raised up the Adventist movement. We have a special message to tell the world. This part of the message is something no one else is talking about, so we should spotlight it.

What the New Testament emphasizes

But there's another principle that we have to keep in mind. There's another principle that needs to inform our perspective: *Christians must emphasize what the New Testament emphasizes.* The New Testament doesn't just lay out an assortment of doctrinal information. It tells us what's most important, what matters most.

Look at what Jesus talked about the most. Look at what Paul talked about the most. Look at what the whole New Testament emphasizes.

In a nutshell, it highlights devotion to Christ and loving one another. It highlights redemption in Christ and spiritual growth in Christ. That's what the New Testament writers talk about at great length. That's what gospel and epistle are centered around.

The investigative judgment doesn't get many lines in the New Testament. Some would even affirm that it doesn't get any. The final judgment is certainly presented, but few explicit details are laid out about the stages, or phases, of that judgment.

I don't believe the New Testament emphasizes the investigative judgment.

I don't believe we should either. That doesn't mean we can't talk about it or preach about it. It simply means this is not central to the Christian faith—so don't *try* to make it central, don't try to make other truths revolve around it.

Healthy religion focuses on what the New Testament emphasizes. Unhealthy religion always focuses on tangents.

I once saw an Adventist booklet that proclaimed that tithing was the essence of Christianity. It very cleverly related all kinds of biblical truths to the principle of tithing.

I believe that's wrong. Jesus is the essence of Christianity. He always was. He always will be. The problem is that you can make a case for almost anything being the essence of Christianity. That's because spiritual things are all interrelated—on the level of abstraction. Love is related to grace, and grace is related to the prayer of reception, and prayer is related to sanctification, and sanctification is related to justification, and justification is related to the judgment. . . . You can go in just about any direction from any one doctrine. I could argue that foot-washing is at the center of all biblical truth or that witnessing is what matters most in the Christian life or that God's sovereignty is the proper starting point for theology. I could make points and use Scripture—but that's not the same as adopting the New Testament's perspective.

Again, what matters is emphasizing what the New Testament emphasizes. We have to keep looking at what the Bible highlights, what stands out most clearly, what stands out to the naked eye—without the filter of commentaries and doctrinal frameworks.

Something happens when a group turns a peripheral truth into a central truth: It always distorts the gospel.

There was a time early in our church when we invested a great deal of theological meaning in the investigative judgment. We made it a key part of salvation. What happened as a result?

We came up with the shut-door theory. We asserted, at a certain point, that the door of probation had closed, that no one else on earth could be saved.

We also came up with the idea that Christ is going to leave His place of intercession just before His return to earth. During that period we will have to stand without a mediator, and every sin will have to be removed from our lives.

And we liked to remind people that we never know when our name may come up in the investigative judgment. Sometimes we alleged that if a person had any unconfessed sin hanging around at that moment, their names would be taken off the book of life.

In other words, we developed beliefs that were almost cultic—some would say altogether cultic—beliefs that we have since revised.

When the investigative judgment was magnified, the truth of justification by faith became small. We tended to forget about Christ covering us with His righteousness. The investigative judgment was a source of constant anxiety to many people, a source of terror. Very few Adventists had an assurance of their standing with God when the investigative judgment loomed large over the horizon.

Yet the New Testament takes pains in passage after passage to give believers just such an assurance. Paul goes to great lengths to help us understand just how sinful human beings are justified before a holy God. He explains to Corinthians, to Galatians, to Ephesians, to Philippians, to Romans—to anyone who will listen—how we can know that we are accepted by God.

How is it that we missed this for so many years? How is it that we didn't get what the New Testament emphasizes? *Because we emphasized something else.*

Think about this: when do you need to be justified by faith? When do you need to be declared righteous before a holy God? In the judgment, of course. That's when this truth of justification by faith has its major application. It's the only way we can make it through the judgment. But Adventists (and others as well) celebrated justification at the beginning of the Christian life and then forgot all about it at the end, the time when we really need it, at the judgment.

When we emphasize what the New Testament doesn't, we always distort the gospel in some way.

Take the Sabbath as another example. I value this day as a gift from God. I probably didn't appreciate it fully until I had kids of my own. But now I look back and see that our best "family times" always happened on Sabbath. And that's when I had the best times with Adventist friends too. There were Sabbaths when the fellowship and the sense of God's blessing were so keen that I felt I was already inhabiting some kind of heavenly time.

Naturally, Adventists proclaim the blessings of the Sabbath. But we do more, much more. We exegete endlessly on the seventh-dayness of the Sabbath, we speculate in book after book on how all the other biblical doctrines relate to the Sabbath, and we theorize on the end-time implications of Sabbath observance.

We make a big deal out of the Sabbath. It's understandable. The Sabbath has been good to us. But again, we have to remember what the New Testament emphasizes. The Sabbath is not central to New Testament theology. Jesus certainly talked about it a lot. But he addressed the issue because He was in hand-to-hand combat against the pervasive legalism of His religious contemporaries. He was trying to get them to lighten up on the Sabbath. It was made for man, not the other way around.

And sometimes it seems we are heaping burdens of our own on the seventh day. We make it carry an incredible load of theological meaning. Sometimes it reminds me of what the Catholic Church has done to the virgin Mary.

Other Christians sometimes feel it necessary to remind Adventists that the Sabbath doesn't save us, Jesus does.

They do that because we divide the world at the end of time into two groups, those who keep the seventh-day Sabbath and those who don't. Naturally people wonder, "What about Jesus, doesn't He count?"

It's impossible to describe how cultic Adventists seem to other Christians when we assert that the genuineness of a believer is determined by which day she or he attends church: You go to church on Saturday, and you have God in your life. You go to church on Sunday, and you don't.

Someone very close to me left the Adventist Church and began attending another congregation in our town. I didn't agree with Jake's decision. He'd left because of an ugly conflict with the church school. There were personal issues I felt he needed to deal with, issues a change in denominations wasn't going to help. But fortunately, Jake ended up in a Bible-based church that has some wonderful worship services. It's perhaps the most dynamic, Christ-centered congregation in our area.

So when I told friends in the Adventist Church about Jake's departure, I tried to soften the blow by explaining that he was still a believer and that he'd found a nurturing, Christian fellowship. But none of that seemed to register. Only the fact that he'd left the correct church mattered. Only the fact that he was now worshiping on the wrong day seemed to count. They offered condolences. They said they would pray for Jake. They acknowledged that he was not yet a completely lost cause.

No one showed the slightest relief that he was still worshiping Christ every week. No one was happy that at least he hadn't rejected God. I wanted to shout, "Isn't this better than if he weren't going to church at all?" It seemed that by switching to the wrong church he'd crossed the line. He was just as "outside" as if he'd started shooting heroin and molesting children.

Healthy religion should give us some perspective. It should help us make subtle judgments. Everything isn't black and white, in or out. Hanging on to God is most important. Attending the correct church is important. But it's not as important as hanging on to God. It's healthy to love your church. It's unhealthy to be unable to see good in other churches.

I believe we make a minor distinction into a major one at our peril. The New Testament simply does not have an involved theology of the Sabbath; Adventists do. That's an important distinction to remember.

Just because a doctrine is unique to us doesn't make it the most important thing in the Bible. Scripture tells us clearly what's most important. We don't have to link together a string of proof texts from Daniel to Revelation in order to find out. God makes it clear: devotion to Christ, love for one another.

Healthy religion emphasizes what the New Testament emphasizes. Unhealthy religion emphasizes pet proof texts. Unhealthy religion impels people to strain out the gnat and swallow the camel. In a compulsive, loveless world, the little things eat up the big things. People are always reacting and overreacting to the enemy. They are continually pushed to extremes.

But a Christian life centered around the devotional study of God's Word creates a different kind of religion, a more open religion. We have a much better chance of developing a healthy perspective as we expose our whole selves—mind, emotions, and spirit—to the whole of God's Word. We'll look more closely at that perspective in the next chapter.

CHAPTER SEVEN

Getting a Sense of Balance

Every time Harold looked out his window at the church across the street, he felt uneasy. Every time he saw the crowds flowing into the auditorium for revival meetings in the evenings, he felt a knot in his stomach. It wasn't that Harold was irreligious. Far from it. He was studying for the ministry at Washington Missionary College, in Maryland. He'd already conducted successful evangelistic campaigns in the Washington, D.C., area. He'd even begun to pastor a church.

What bothered Harold was the man those crowds were going in to hear. He was one of the most gifted speakers in the church, a union president. But a conflict had flared up between him and Harold's father, a conference president. Harold's mother was also involved, because she headed departments within the conference. Dad and Mom would never breathe a word about their problems to Harold, but he found out through other people. And he came to believe that his parents had been wronged and that this church official had bad-mouthed his mother.

That's pretty hard for the devoted son of godly parents to take. Harold had never hated another human being in his life. But he found that animosity toward this man was growing like a cancer in his heart. He felt it every time he glanced out the window of the tiny attic apartment in the large house on campus where he lived. He felt it when he rose at four in the morning to start the coal furnace in the basement and heat up the house for the other tenants.

The warmth wasn't reaching inside him. Nothing melted the icy block of outrage over what this man spouting revival across the street, this high and mighty official, had done.

And there was something else that intensified Harold's anguish even further. He was scheduled to be ordained into the gospel ministry in a few weeks. And one of the people who would be presiding at this ordination, one of the people who would be placing a hand on his head in blessing, was the union president, the man he despised.

Harold knew he couldn't permit himself to be ordained while harboring this hatred. As he recalled: "Something had to get into me and change me— whatever happened to him." And yet his beloved parents had been dishonored. How could he just let that go?

Harold prayed for days up in his attic room, struggling through his "dark night of the soul." And finally he found a way out.

One evening Harold slowly walked down the stairs, across the street, and into the church auditorium. He sat and listened to his enemy's sermon. And at the end of it, when this man gave an altar call, Harold walked down the aisle to the front and stood with those weeping for their sins.

After everyone else had gone, Harold introduced himself to the speaker. He told this man all about what he'd been feeling and why. He confessed his hatred.

The church official broke down right there and acknowledged that he hadn't acted fairly toward Harold's parents. Harold recalled, "We got our arms around each other and got our tears all mixed up together. And a strange thing happened. From that time on, I considered him one of my best friends. We became very close."

This young preacher went on to build a wonderfully successful radio ministry called *The Voice of Prophecy*. But Harold—H. M. S. Richards, Sr.— would never forget that moment of truth: "It changed my whole life. It gave me a new start and a new vision of everything. I *knew* that God can take care of sin in your life. I've been through it. I've seen Him do it."

Pastor Richards suggests a clear alternative to the religion of having to be right. And his experience shows us how liberating that alternative can be. There are a thousand different ways to hide our faults. We can develop endless ways of pointing "the truth" at everyone else but ourselves. And all these things prove exhausting in the end; they burn us out. But there's just one way of turning in the other direction: *honestly admitting that we are wrong.*

God's right; I'm forgiven

Unhealthy religion is a vehicle for being head-right when you're heart-wrong. Healthy religion has a very different starting point: we are all wrong, we all fall short of the glory of God. But God cherishes us anyway. He desires our companionship; He finds something redeemable in us; He nurtures our faith.

The catch is that people have an extremely hard time admitting they are wrong or weak when they don't feel loved and accepted. It may seem, on the surface, that the opposite should be true, that those who feel emptiest inside should have the easiest time acknowledging they are sinners before God. But the fact is you have to be loved in order to see yourself as a sinner, a needy person. Christ's awesome demonstration of grace on the cross precedes our coming to Him in repentance. Without love you have to keep covering up. You keep trying to be more right than your neighbor. You can't afford to admit that you're weak and prone to error.

Other people sometimes work very hard to prove to individuals who have to be right that they are wrong, that their perspective is askew. But that only makes them argue more passionately for their position. They instinctively feel that if they're not right, they're not anything. And so they will go to great lengths to keep from being argued right out of existence.

Only love can break down defenses. Only divine love can take us to the right starting point.

The right starting point is justification by faith. That's the process by which God bestows the verdict of innocence on people who keep falling short. But this doctrine needs to become much more than just a proper explanation of how we are saved. It needs to become a working principle in our own hearts. It needs to sink in.

To be a Christian is to first drop our defenses, to admit that we are wrong, thoroughly imperfect. We each stand before an awesome, holy God. "Even the moon is not bright and the stars are not pure in his eyes" (Job 25:5). Before God's righteousness, our goodness looks like filthy rags. When confronted with His law, we become conscious of our weakness. His glory makes us aware of how far we've fallen from holiness.

Only God is 100 percent right 100 percent of the time. Our human struggle to be right, to justify ourselves, is a lost cause. It's foolish to try to force someone else to acknowledge our rightness when God has shown that we are desperately sick.

We need to realize that the war is over and we've lost. Struggling to be counted right—by our associates at work, by fellow church members, by our spouses—is like the Japanese soldier on a forgotten island in the Pacific who continued his guerrilla fighting twenty years after armistice.

Before God we are wrong. This destroys the basic assumption of the who-is-right argument: Two people must compete for a limited amount of rightness; one person must be right and the other wrong. Each individual on this seesaw tries to bring the other down and push himself up. If you're down, I'm up—and vice versa. We go bobbing up and down endlessly on the leverage of our little debates. It's a childish game played in dead earnest.

Justification demands that we all begin on the same side of the seesaw. Before God, we're all on the down side. Our frail goodness has no uplifting leverage. One person may win an argument, but that really leads nowhere.

Recognizing how wrong we are, however, is no cause for despair. It's the first step in finding true rightness and security. Jesus died for the ungodly, and justification comes only to sinners. God invites us to come to Him, confess our wrongness, and receive His pardon.

When we place our faith in God, He regards us as righteous. Christ's perfect obedience displaces our disobedience. We are accepted in the Beloved.

Because of this divine acceptance, we can cheerfully admit that we are wrong. God gives us security despite our wrongness. We are no longer under pressure to rack up I-was-right points.

Paul could freely confess his serious mistakes because he understood his standing with God. He didn't try to excuse his early persecution of the church, although at the time he sincerely believed that hunting down members of the Jesus sect was right. Instead, Paul presented himself as the worst of sinners on whom God had lavished grace.

How refreshing it would be to reply, when accused: "Yes, it's quite possible I'm wrong. I'm thoroughly imperfect and make mistakes easily. That's why I have to depend on God for any consistent rightness."

God sees our weaknesses and yet values us as His children. No one, in fact, penetrates our hearts more deeply—yet, no one believes in us so ardently. Knowing this should make it easier to be vulnerable before others. Surely if I can acknowledge the deceitfulness of my heart before God Almighty, I can also admit that I misinterpreted that text about the millennium last week in Sabbath School class.

Justification creates a totally new kind of rightness. Our buoyant new identity raises us up with Christ. We are seated with Him in heavenly realms. We enter the Most Holy Place where God is enthroned with confidence.

This rightness qualifies us to "share in the inheritance of the saints in the kingdom of light" (Colossians 1:12). We have an advocate before the Father who pleads our case.

Paul considered his credentials as a "faultless" Pharisee mere rubbish compared to righteousness provided by grace. Throughout his letters he insisted that only this rightness is worth having; trying to establish some other right-standing wars against the gospel.

We don't have to seize every tidbit of "I told you so" for some assurance of being right. As well as being cheerfully wrong, we can be quietly right. Why wrestle so hard for superior status in our church or before other believers whom we prove wrong? We already enjoy the most privileged position in Christ.

Getting wrapped up in proving ourselves correct shows we've lost sight of our true standing. Why work so hard at defending ourselves when we have such a competent attorney in Jesus Christ? Fighting to be right, like warring for peace, is a contradiction in terms.

Condemn less, listen more

The truth of justification by faith is meant to inform our whole perspective on life. Being "right" in Christ not only can make us more able to admit our imperfections; it also can make us more able to listen to other people. Other believers are "right" in Christ too. Yes, they're imperfect just as we are. But God is focusing on their faith. God is focusing on their potential. We should be too. And God is giving them more and more insights into His truth. They sometimes see things we don't. So we can learn something important from them.

The religion of having to be right, however, only applies the truth of justification by faith to me or my group—if at all: I may be imperfect, but God is guiding me; God is leading me into all truth. But acknowledging that God may be guiding other people even though they are doctrinally imperfect is another matter. It's easier to assume that the devil is behind those who disagree with us. It's easier to assume that one error makes the other guy's movement counterfeit.

There's a clear alternative to this kind of unhealthy isolation. There's a clear alternative to demonizing the flaws of others. It's something simple. It's something called being teachable. We have something important to learn from believers who are different from us. We have things to learn from Christian groups who are different from us. We're all flawed. We're all vulnerable.

So make discoveries through other people! God has something to teach you in the brother that you discount so easily. You probably need some of what he has too much of. And he probably needs some of what you have too much of. Become teachable. That's how we get out of our ruts.

Healthy religion is teachable religion. People learn from those who are different. They don't just demonize them. They become more balanced as they take in various perspectives. They learn that truth often grows in unexpected places.

Successful evangelists—those who make a career out of dispensing truth in no uncertain terms—don't often suggest to us models of teachableness. When you're seeing multitudes moved by your powerful oratory, it's easy for your ego to get inflated. Someone who's a perpetual proclaimer seems least likely to listen well.

But H. M. S. Richards, Sr. became a model of teachableness. He had a wonderful capacity to appreciate the gifts of other ministers. You can hear that in an interview made in his library as he's looking over several volumes of Spurgeon's sermons and commenting, "He was the greatest Bible preacher since Paul." You can hear that when he talks of George Whitefield holding vast crowds captive to the Word of God. Richards liked to tell of Ben Franklin emptying his pockets before going to hear Whitefield preach. Because he knew that when this man began to plead for money for his orphanage in Georgia, he would give everything he had.

And Richards also liked to tell a story that is a great commentary on his own life. When Whitefield died, a great memorial service was held at which John Wesley preached. These two men had worked together but sharply disagreed on the doctrine of once-saved-always-saved. And many thought that this had made them enemies.

After the funeral sermon, a woman approached Wesley and asked, "Do you think you'll see George Whitefield in heaven?"

Wesley replied, "I'm afraid I won't."

This seemed to make the woman almost gleeful. "I knew it. I knew in spite of all you said that you hated him."

"You don't understand," Wesley interrupted. "I think when I get to heaven, Brother Whitefield will be so near the throne of God's glory that I'll never catch sight of him."

H. M. S. Richards, Sr. shared that kind of gracious spirit. Commenting on this anecdote, he said with great feeling: "That's the way preachers ought to feel about each other. If a man can come into town and paint a better picture than I can, I can really praise Him because I don't know how to paint. If he can make a better car, I can praise him because I don't know how to use those tools.

"But if he can beat me at preaching or radio work, I've got to have the grace of God not to damn him with faint praise. That's a great test of us. If a man can do our job better than we can, we ought to pray for God to give us grace to really pray and shed tears of joy—here's a man who can do it better than I can—and back him up with all our hearts."

Richards could preach what he felt was the truth forcefully, without apology. But he didn't allow doctrinal differences to narrow his heart.

Dwight L. Moody, one of the most prolific evangelists of modern times, also developed a remarkably teachable attitude. This man who could shoot straight about sin and salvation to receptive crowds on both sides of the Atlantic could also respond humbly when God shot straight at him.

During one long preaching tour, Moody was traveling by train with a singer named Towner. A drunk with a badly bruised eye recognized the famous evangelist and started bawling out hymns. The weary Moody didn't want to deal with the man and suggested, "Let's get out of here." But Towner told him that all the other cars were full.

When a conductor came down the aisle, Moody stopped him and pointed out the drunk. The conductor gently quieted the man, bathed and bandaged his eye, and then led him back to a seat where he could fall asleep.

After reflecting on all this for a while, Moody told his companion, "Towner, this has been a terrible rebuke for me! I preached last night to that crowd against Pharisaism and exhorted them to imitate the Good Samaritan, and now this morning God has given me an opportunity to practice what I preached and I find I have both feet in the shoes of the priest and Levite." Moody included this story against himself in his messages during the rest of the tour.

In an age when fathers exercised an often tyrannical authority in the household and children existed to be ordered around, Moody endeared himself to his sons Will and Paul by his easy playfulness and by acknowledging his weaknesses. His daughter-in-law remembered, "Oh yes, he had a quick temper, but my husband's and Paul's great memory of their father was when he had lost his temper with them, and after they had gone to bed they would hear those heavy footsteps and he'd come into their room and put a heavy hand on their head and say, 'I want you to forgive me, that wasn't the way Christ taught.' "

Moody was a man of enormous drive who built churches, seminaries, training schools, sponsored conferences, and managed to unite quarrelsome church groups for great evangelistic endeavors. A riddle of the time: "Why is D. L. so good? Because he drives so fast the devil can't catch him." But unlike many powerful religious leaders who come to see their every enterprise as de facto God's will, Moody remained sensitive to direction.

When the devastating Chicago fire of 1871 destroyed his church and mission school, Moody did not assume the typical posture: "This is the devil's attack on my righteous cause." He tried to listen a little more carefully. Later he recalled, "The Chicago Fire was the turning point of my life. I had become so mixed up with building Farwell Hall and was on committees of every kind of work, and in my ambition to make my enterprises succeed because they were mine I had taken my eyes off from the Lord and had been burdened in soul and unfruitful in my work. When the Fire came, as a revelation, I took my hat and walked out!"

Moody the celebrity managed to stay teachable. He wanted to keep learning. A friend once noted Moody "seems to carry about with him now a little library; how he can have time to read, I cannot think." One of his favorite phrases was "We must grow or go to the wall."

In his travels, says one biographer, Moody "always soaked up information on local background and personalities, pumped people about their families and work and interests." He read the daily papers faithfully, being deeply interested in political and international affairs. But unlike many of his contemporaries who glibly pontificated from the pulpit on issues they knew little about, Moody refused to press his opinions. He said he simply couldn't study enough to make legitimate public comment.

Moody, the teachable proclaimer, remained so until the end. Instead of dominating the annual General Workers' Conference which he had labored so hard to create, Moody invited the best men he could find to teach. After introducing a speaker, he would leave the platform and sit at his feet, a colleague recalled, "always with his Bible open, always with a pen or pencil in his hand, and if anything was said which was particularly good he noted it and used it without hesitation." A seminary president fondly remembered: "When I opened to him the Bible which was so precious to him, the tears would come to his eyes and he would say, 'Say that again, Doctor.' "

Moody was continually awed by the transformations he saw God work in people's lives. He never reduced the Almighty to the size of his own group, his own following. He always realized that God's work in the world was more vast than he could imagine. When a group of ministers were debating which speaker to invite to their meetings, one suggested they call D. L. Moody.

Another was a bit miffed: "Does Moody have a monopoly on the Holy Spirit?"

His colleague replied, "No, but the Holy Spirit has a monopoly on Moody."

The bottom line is love

After we have begun to honestly admit our imperfect grasp of the truth, after we have developed a teachable spirit, we need to do one more thing. We need to make sure that in all our adding up of doctrinal truths, in all our gathering of texts, in all our proclamation of biblical insights—the bottom line is love. That is, if the sum of what we assert as truth doesn't become love in someone's heart, then we're just a noisy gong or a clanging cymbal.

The New Testament urges us to speak the truth in love, because bad things happen when truth is separated from love. It starts taking all those dysfunctional detours we examined in the last two chapters. It gets puffed up. It stakes out turf to defend at all costs. It majors in minor details.

God's truth is something that nurtures human beings. It doesn't burn us out. It builds us up. The truth of the New Testament is bathed in God's lavish grace. There's hardly a verse in the epistles that isn't explaining or magnifying it. The apostles are always talking about how we can receive it more deeply or share it more widely.

Grace is an experience. Genuine truth can never be just an exercise for the mind, just a matter of getting religious equations in proper order. It has to be something that echoes in our hearts. While it's true that we don't discover God's truth solely by what we feel is right, it's also true that we don't truly discover God's truth until we feel it's right. After the head acknowledges that God's revelation makes good sense, after we see the logical coherence of the gospel and the plan of salvation, we need to open up our hearts so that gospel can touch us on an emotional level. Beautiful things can happen as a result. Beautiful things can happen when we know in our hearts, as well as in our heads, that the bottom line is love.

Pastor Glenn Coon was a remarkable example of what can happen when a man centers his ministry around God's grace. He grew up in a time when the essentials of the gospel weren't all that well championed in the Adventist Church. On the surface he appeared the spitting image of conservative religious goodness, thoroughly conventional. His dress and language and mannerisms were those of that older generation of church leaders who had battled over whether wedding rings constituted jewelry or not and what the appropriate response was to being offered "unclean meats" at someone's house and generally tied down every loose end of life with a paragraph in the church manual.

Pastor Coon followed rather strict standards, but they did not define him; that did not become his truth. He expressed something bigger and more animated. When this pastor spoke, people's hearts burned with the love of Jesus; somehow he managed to turn that cliché into a very present reality.

Glenn Coon had a theme, something to express. He kept proclaiming it over and over: Jesus believes in us, hopes for us, loves us, forgives us; that's how we must relate to each other. Christ's gracious regard was so powerfully real to Coon that it overshadowed all other factors that influence relationships. It was something that just *had* to be expressed. And so he found a very fruitful ministry among the many on the road to burnout.

Once one of Pastor Coon's church members, a man we'll call Ralph, left his wife and children. He went to a nearby city and rented an apartment for himself. This, of course, caused quite an uproar in the church. One of the elders came to Pastor Coon and exclaimed, "You know, *that* man must be dealt with at once." The inference was that Ralph needed to be strongly disciplined, perhaps disfellowshiped right away.

Well, the pastor promised he would phone Ralph and make an appointment. But the elder thought that was a terrible idea. "Call him on the telephone?" he said. "Why I should say not! If he knows you want to talk with him, you'll *never* get to see him. The only way to get to see *that* man is to come on him suddenly, like cornering a lion in his den."

Pastor Glenn thanked the elder for his concern and then, after much prayer, called Ralph. And this is how he began the conversation: "Ralph, I'm your new pastor. I have some *wonderful* news for you! Something you will like very much. But I have to see you alone. I'd like to meet you in my car, in my driveway, so we can be entirely alone."

Well, this "fallen church member" who'd been declared all but unreachable quickly agreed to come. He promised, "I'll be there tonight." And sure enough, at the appointed time, Ralph walked up to Pastor Coon's driveway and stepped into the front seat of his car.

The minister turned to him and said enthusiastically. "I have something wonderful for you, as I said. It's nothing financial, but I've come to bring you victory over sin."

At the words, "victory over sin," Ralph seemed to slump down in his seat. He stared out the window into the darkness. The man seemed to be wondering, "Is this pastor just trying to gather information to use against me?"

Pastor Coon continued talking, assuring Ralph of his genuine concern and of his experience in dealing confidentially with similar problems. He mentioned other people he'd known who had come out victorious after serious moral failures.

The minister talked for thirty minutes, forty minutes, and still there was no response. But he persisted in hope, saying he was a friend who was there to help Ralph. "I know you can be saved," he said. "I believe you *will* be saved."

Suddenly Ralph dropped his head and began to sob like a child. He turned to the minister and said, "Pastor, I don't believe there is any hope for me."

Pastor Coon put his arm around him and quoted 1 John 1:9: "If we confess our sins, he is faithful and just and will forgive us our sins and purify us from all unrighteousness."

Pastor Coon was fanning that tiny spark of hope. He continued presenting Scripture promises about God's acceptance, forgiveness, cleansing, and rest. And he added fervently, "Jesus is bringing you victory *now*. You *are* His child. You *are* turning to God."

The pastor, now weeping himself, was so moved by faith that he told Ralph about the great work for God this man could do in the future. Suddenly Ralph raised up his head and looked the minister in the eye. "Brother Coon," he said, "I'm going home."

Faith had produced its wonderful fruit. Ralph had seized that ray of hope. Pastor Coon was, of course, overjoyed and received the assurance that Ralph would return to his wife and children the very next day.

That meant the pastor had time to go and prepare the wife for this homecoming. Early the next morning he hurried over and told her, as enthusiastically as possible, "Jo Ann, your husband was converted last night, and he is coming home. And he is going to serve the Lord."

This woman looked back at the pastor as though she could eat nails and replied with a sneer, "Oh yeah! He *needs* to be converted! You think *he* is!"

Pastor Coon's heart just about sunk through the floor. He saw his victory of hope melting away before his eyes. But the minister bravely pressed on. "Yes," he told Jo Ann, "God came in last night in a wonderful way, and the Holy Spirit melted your husband's heart."

"Hmm!" the woman shot back, "Better melt it! Better melt it!"

Now it was getting harder and harder for this minister to keep

showing faith. He was greatly tempted to give this woman's sneer right back to her. *Anything but a Pharisee!* he thought. *What* can *you do for a self-satisfied religionist?*

Pastor Coon felt like walking right out the door. But then he remembered his encounter with Ralph the previous night. He'd expressed faith—and God had acted. Couldn't this woman benefit from confidence expressed in her as well? The pastor shot a quick prayer heavenward asking God to help him inspire Jo Ann with hope.

And then he found the strength to say these words: "Jo Ann, do you know what you are going to do when your husband comes home? I'm going to make a prediction. You'll rush out on the front porch and throw your arms around him. You'll give him the warmest welcome of his life. He needs it, and it will mean his salvation."

Jo Ann's reply shocked even this pastor who was trying so hard to hope. The woman's sneer disappeared, a light came on in her eyes, and she declared, "That's *just* what I'm going to do." Pastor Coon could scarcely believe what he'd heard, but he recovered enough to suggest they kneel down and pray together. The two joyfully gave thanks to God for what He'd done.

A few days after his conversations with Ralph and Jo Ann, Pastor Coon spotted their son in a grocery store. The minister edged over to where the boy was picking up a few items, bent down and asked quietly, "How is everything at your home?"

The boy immediately straightened up tall and said with a beaming face, "Daddy's back home!"

Glenn Coon could have easily burned out or at least burned low over the years after his many encounters with the casualties of the religion of having to be right. But through five decades of ministry, he inspired audiences with a simple straightforward account of the matchless love of Christ. When Coon spoke about such things, it was not the same old story. It came alive. He was continually rejuvenated by the essentials of New Testament faith: devotion to Christ and love for one another. And he made those qualities very real in the countless lives he touched.

Summary of Part II

Healthy Religion Seeks Wisdom

Acknowledges weaknesses

"God have mercy on me, a sinner" (Luke 18:13).

For that very reason I was shown mercy so that in me, the worst of sinners, Christ Jesus might display his unlimited patience . . . (1 Timothy 1:16).

Sees its need

Create in me a pure heart, O God, and renew a steadfast spirit within me (Psalm 51:10).

Appreciates true wisdom

The wisdom that comes from heaven is first of all pure; then peace-loving, considerate, submissive, full of mercy and good fruit, impartial and sincere (James 3:17).

Unhealthy Religion Seeks Argument

Has to be right

If you rely on the law and brag about your relationship to God; . . . if you are convinced that you are a guide for the blind, a light for those who are in the dark, . . . because you have in the law the embodiment of knowledge and truth—you, then, who teach others, do you not teach yourself? (Romans 2:17-21).

Never sees its real need

"We are Abraham's descendants and have never been slaves of anyone. How can you say that we shall be set free?" (John 8:33).

"If you were blind, you would not be guilty of sin; but now that you claim you can see, your guilt remains" (John 9:41).

Deifies personal opinion

Do not let anyone who delights in false humility and the worship of angels disqualify you for the prize. Such a person goes into great detail about what he has seen, and his unspiritual mind puffs him up with idle notions. He has lost connection with the Head (Colossians 2:18, 19).

Healthy Religion Seeks Wisdom

Engages in winsome conversation

Let your conversation be always full of grace, seasoned with salt, so that you may know how to answer everyone (Colossians 4:6).

Healthy Religion Understands

Understands what's most important

"If you are offering your gift at the altar and there remember that your brother has something against you, leave your gift there in front of the altar. First go and be reconciled to your brother; then come and offer your gift" (Matthew 5:23, 24).

Emphasizes what the New Testament emphasizes

I resolved to know nothing while I was with you except Jesus Christ and him crucified (1 Corinthians 2:2).

The goal of this command is love, which comes from a pure heart and a good conscience and a sincere faith (1 Timothy 1:5).

Unhealthy Religion Seeks Argument

Is compelled to argue

He has an unhealthy interest in controversies and quarrels about words that result in envy, strife, malicious talk, evil suspicions and constant friction between men of corrupt mind (1 Timothy 6:4, 5).

Unhealthy Religion Distorts

Can't make fine distinctions

The Lord answered him, "You hypocrites! Doesn't each of you on the Sabbath untie his ox or donkey from the stall and lead it out to give it water? Then should not this woman, a daughter of Abraham, whom Satan has kept bound for eighteen long years, be set free on the Sabbath day from what bound her?" (Luke 13:15, 16).

Gets off on tangents

Command certain men not to teach false doctrines any longer nor to devote themselves to myths and endless genealogies. These promote controversies rather than God's work—which is by faith (1 Timothy 1:3, 4).

Develops insight

This is my prayer: that your love may abound more and more in knowledge and depth of insight, so that you may be able to discern what is best (Philippians 1:9,10).

Gets its bearings from the gospel

We have peace with God through our Lord Jesus Christ, through whom we have gained access by faith into this grace in which we now stand (Romans 5:1, 2).

Stand firm, then, and do not let yourselves be burdened again by a yoke of slavery (Galatians 5:1).

Healthy Religion Keeps Learning

Is teachable

Show me your ways, O Lord, teach me your paths; guide me in your truth and teach me, for you are God my Savior, and my hope is in you all day long (Psalm 25:4, 5).

Lacks perspective

You are looking only on the surface of things (2 Corinthians 10:7).

Distorts the gospel

I declare to every man who lets himself be circumcised that he is obligated to obey the whole law. You who are trying to be justified by law have been alienated from Christ; you have fallen away from grace.... For in Christ Jesus neither circumcision nor uncircumcision has any value. The only thing that counts is faith expressing itself through love (Galatians 5:3, 4, 6).

Unhealthy Religion Keeps Blind Spots
Can't take criticism

And [Jesus] said, "Is it not written: " 'My house will be called a house of prayer for all nations'? But you have made it 'a den of robbers.' " The chief priests and the teachers of the law . . . began looking for a way to kill him (Mark 11:17, 18).

"You are determined to kill me, a man who has told you the truth.... You are doing the things your own father does." "We are not illegitimate children," they protested. "The only Father we have is God himself" (John 8:40, 41).

Healthy Religion Keeps Learning	**Unhealthy Religion Keeps Blind Spots**

Healthy Religion Keeps Learning

Listens

The Sovereign Lord has given me an instructed tongue, to know the word that sustains the weary. He wakens me morning by morning, wakens my ear to listen like one being taught. The Sovereign Lord has opened my ears, and I have not been rebellious; I have not drawn back (Isaiah 50:4, 5).

Sees God working good out of imperfection

Some preach Christ out of envy and rivalry . . . But what does it matter? The important thing is that in every way, whether from false motives or true, Christ is preached. And because of this I rejoice (Philippians 1:15, 18).

Absorbs truth on a deeper level

I pray also that the eyes of your heart may be enlightened (Ephesians 1:18).

Unhealthy Religion Keeps Blind Spots

Never really gets it

"They have eyes to see but do not see and ears to hear but do not hear" (Ezekiel 12:2).

"You blind guides! You strain out a gnat but swallow a camel" (Matthew 23:24).

The light shines in the darkness, but the darkness has not understood it (John 1:5).

Sees a supposed imperfection ruining the whole

Philip found Nathanael and told him, "We have found the one Moses wrote about . . . Jesus of Nazareth, the son of Joseph."

"Nazareth! Can anything good come from there?" Nathanael asked (John 1:45, 46).

"He is worthy of death," they answered (Matthew 26:65, 66).

Looks at reality through a filter

Their minds were made dull, for to this day the same veil remains when the old covenant is read. It has not been removed, because only in Christ is it taken away. Even to this day when Moses is read, a veil covers their hearts (2 Corinthians 3:14, 15).

Learns in humility

"Therefore, whoever humbles himself like this child is the greatest in the kingdom of heaven" (Matthew 18:4).

"You are not to be called 'Rabbi,' for you have only one Master and you are all brothers (Matthew 23:8).

Like newborn babies, crave pure spiritual milk, so that by it you may grow up in your salvation, now that you have tasted that the Lord is good (1 Peter 2:2, 3).

Is blinded by pride

They boast about themselves and flatter others for their own advantage (Jude 16).

Some Pharisees . . . asked, "What? Are we blind too?" Jesus said, "If you were blind, you would not be guilty of sin; but now that you claim you can see, your guilt remains" (John 9:40, 41).

The Church:
Us Versus Them

CHAPTER Eight

Are You Suspicious of Joy?

It appeared at first like a very deep analysis, this critique of the "celebration movement" from a religious journal that someone had copied and placed in my hands. The author, a pastor and teacher, didn't just deal with drums and people raising their hands. He zeroed in on the theological issues behind what he identified as a new attempt, within Adventism, to receive the Holy Spirit.

But within a few paragraphs the man stated categorically that it's not possible to remain neutral about celebration. It isn't part good and bad. You have to choose between Christ and Barabbas; it's either a work of God or a work of Satan.

Well, that took me back a bit. I don't know of any religious movement in history that has not had elements of good and bad in it. After all, these are human beings, not angels, who are involved.

Still, some movements have been almost all bad, quite destructive psychologically, so I read on. The man first considered the timing of the "celebration movement." He affirmed that we are living in a time of crisis, prefigured by the Day of Atonement in the Old Testament, when the Hebrews were called to purify their hearts and lament for their sins.

The writer concluded that those facing the close of probation need to be afflicting their souls. He couldn't see how anyone could possibly celebrate when there was such "widespread apostasy" in the church. What we need instead is the kind of "straight testimony" that John the Baptist gave.

The article emphasized what a terrible mistake it is to celebrate when God calls for deep repentance, and it identified "this rebellion" as a sin that cannot be pardoned.

Now I was starting to get upset. I realized this man was claiming that the worship of the Adventist Church in our time had to be dominated by repentance and mourning—or we would be in rebellion against God. There was only one way to worship correctly—and it had nothing to do with celebration.

It's one thing to say that some individuals party when they should be weeping over their sins. Moments of truth come in each of our lives when we have to face the more serious music of the Holy Spirit. And we shouldn't drown out that conviction with frivolity.

But to assert that this solemn introspection should characterize all Adventist worship, all of the time, in every congregation—boggles the mind. What a reductionist picture of the Christian life! Everything is suddenly melted down to one element: mourning. That's incredibly unhealthy. People can't sustain that. It's a major highway to burnout.

The Adventist movement began largely as a means of preparing people for the judgment, making people aware of the end times in which we are living. The "time of crisis" that the writer referred to has existed since the mid-1800s. So should we have been mourning and afflicting ourselves Sabbath after Sabbath for 150 years? Should generations have grown up in our churches and have known nothing but this kind of worship? I tremble to think of the kind of pathological human beings that would have produced.

Scripture asks us to mourn for sin. Jesus says those who do are blessed. But Scripture also demands that we rejoice in the Lord always. It asks us to bless His name continually. It asks us to repent and lift up our hearts in praises. It asks us to search our hearts and to exult in the Lord and raise a joyful noise that echoes out into the heavens.

In other words, healthy worship involves our whole selves as whole human beings. It involves, at various times, the whole spectrum of our emotions. The worship of the Lord of the universe can bring out our tears and our laughter, our fondest whispers and our most excited shouts, our deepest thoughts and our strongest energies.

Unhealthy worship always reduces God to one dimension—the dimension that we're accustomed to.

Some people are just not very expressive. Their melancholy temperament has made them introspective and solemn. That's OK. But it's not OK to create a picture of God out of that limited personality and demand that others bow down to it. It's not OK to create worship in your image and demand that others follow it or be damned as rebellious.

We all need to lighten up. We need to let other people worship in their own way and express praises in the way most natural for them. We need to learn from other people's exuberance, just as they may need to learn something from our introspection. We picture a bigger God when we picture Him all together.

Some people don't have a lot of love pouring out from their hearts. They never got much of it growing up, perhaps. That's not their fault. But it's not OK to create a loveless worship out of that emptiness. It's even worse to decree that kind of worship for others.

When we don't feel love from God, we don't feel like pouring our praises back to Him. We're cut off from that kind of joyful noise. The only thing we can do is furrow our brows and grit our teeth and try harder to please Him. Mourning and afflicting our hearts come naturally. It's all part of that chronic sense of insecurity and inadequacy. It's not just a response to conviction. It's a response to our dysfunction.

That's the bottom line behind a lot of theological smoke that has blown up around this or that kind of worship. People may think they're waging a battle for the truth or for the pure church. But too often they're just documenting the narrowness of their hearts. They instinctively want everyone else to fit into their painfully limited worship repertoire. They can't bear the idea of others exulting freely in the Lord when they can only mourn. It doesn't seem that these celebrants can possibly have genuine religion. The chronic mourners have labored so long and hard in their attempts to serve the Lord—with so little joy to show for it. Surely it can't be true that joy could fall so abundantly on others who are so much less worthy.

Healthy religion wells up with joy.

Unhealthy religion is instinctively suspicious of joy.

The Pharisees seem to have opposed joy every time they met it. When Jesus replaced merchants and money-changers at the temple with the blind and the lame, whom He healed, officials became indignant. The street urchins shouting "Hosanna" made them especially upset. Jesus answered their criticism with a quote, "From the lips of children and infants you have ordained praise."

When the Pharisees spotted a former paralytic delirious with joy over the fact that thirty-eight years of misery had suddenly slunk away under Jesus' touch and turned into perfect health, the only thing they noticed was that he carried a mat under his arm on the Sabbath. More indignation.

When a man who'd never seen a sunrise or a fig tree or a baby's skin in all his life was brought before them testifying "I was blind but now I see!" they managed to get bent out of shape because the healer had made mud on the Sabbath to put on his eyes.

During Christ's triumphal entry into Jerusalem, the crowd was beside themselves shouting praises. Pharisees frowning over the festive scene demanded that Jesus rebuke His noisy disciples. "I tell you," he replied, "if they keep quiet, the stones will cry out."

God kept wanting the Pharisees to rejoice because the prodigal son had come home at last, the lost sheep had been found, the unchosen had become chosen. But they, the elder brothers, couldn't stop mumbling and grumbling because they had worked so hard all these years—and apparently had received so little.

Healthy religion wells up with praise. Healthy religion thrives on thankfulness. Unhealthy religion can never quite get beyond the struggle to make it; it can never quite get beyond its secret fear and resentment.

Negative people create unhealthy religion. They may think they are champions of righteousness, called as watchmen to point out the sins creeping into the church. But they're just processing the negative emotions inside them. They're stuck on the bad stuff. They keep pointing out sins because there's nothing else to point to.

Negative people may think they are called to alert the church to all kinds of dangers and plots and conspiracies out in the world that fit into some master end-times plan. They may think they have special insight into all the calamities that are building up to one huge time of trouble. (And they may on occasion be right.) But mostly, they're just expressing their negative view of life. They see calamities everywhere because of the calamity in their hearts. Their gloomy predictions may seem pious, but these are mostly an expression of the permanent shadows in their hearts.

Negative people may think they have a responsibility to give "the straight testimony." They may think that their chronic criticisms come straight from "present truth." But mostly, they come straight from their unhappy temperament. Chronic criticism is a way of venting the ugliness or emptiness inside.

Negative people create unhealthy religion. It's something that needs to be confronted in the church. Negative people shouldn't be in charge; they shouldn't be the voices we obey. We shouldn't mistake intimidation for conviction. We shouldn't mistake bluntness for insight. We shouldn't mistake someone who seems stricter than us for someone who is closer to God than us.

One reason this is such an important issue is that joyless worship drives people away from church. They stop coming. They burn out on the endless solemnity. They burn out after years of boring church services.

In this chapter we're going to look at key factors in the quality of worship services that can either build us up or burn us out, key factors that determine whether our worship is essentially joyful or not. In the Adventist Church, we've been careful to assure that congregations adhere to our fundamental beliefs, that we are everywhere affirming the same truths—from Sydney to Bangkok, from St. Petersburg to Toronto. That's a good thing. What is much harder to assure is the quality of our worship services, the actual experience of church. But that is also vitally important.

Individuals are nurtured when church becomes an experience that lifts them up, that makes them feel closer to God. That experience keeps them going in the Christian life. Sitting in the pew can be a statement of allegiance to a certain denomination. That's fine. But we need more than that to make worship sustainable and rewarding. We need to look at the bottom line: What is worship like in the Adventist Church? What are people actually getting out of our services? We need to look carefully not just at doctrinal error but also at flaws that greatly affect the quality of worship.

Here are three of the more serious impediments to spiritual joy in our churches:

Discussing instead of sharing

I've been fortunate enough to have had some great times of fellowship. On occasion, I've been able to deeply bond with other believers as we shared about the things that matter most. I remember pouring my heart out to a buddy as we struggled with similar temptations. We were in the good fight together. It was great to have someone who understood. I remember the excitement of talking about witnessing and experiencing it with other kids in college. We felt as though we were in a great movement together.

But I'm disturbed that those times of fellowship have almost never coincided with my lifelong church attendance as an Adventist. In other words, I haven't found much fellowship in the one place where fellowship is supposed to happen.

Take Sabbath School classes, for example. Here you have the perfect setting for a time of meaningful sharing between brothers and sisters in Christ: a small group studying the Word together. This should be a terrific opportunity for mutual encouragement and support.

But what happens in a typical Sabbath School class? Week after week, year after year, these sessions are dominated by abstract discussion, talk of principles, review of doctrine.

People make points, people share their views, people talk about their interpretation of a passage. People talk about all kinds of things—except *life*. That is, no one talks about their real life in Sabbath School—what's going on, what they're struggling with, what they're happy or distressed about.

We do very well on the theoretical level. We talk at great length about how we should grow as Christians, tossing about all kinds of theories about sanctification. But no one talks about how they are growing, or failing to grow, as a Christian.

Instead, we address topics. Is there such a thing as healthy pride? We can discuss what humility is or isn't in detail, but no one talks about their struggle with insecurity or egotism.

We can debate the basis for a believer's assurance of salvation and the fine line between presumption and faith. But no one shares secret fears about their standing with God because they keep on falling for the same old sin.

We can discuss the need to witness, the whys of witnessing, the hows of witnessing, the biblical basis for witnessing. But people rarely talk about what worked and what didn't when they actually witnessed.

Sometimes, sitting there in the pew with my nice suit on and my nice face on, I want to scream: "Somebody tell me what's going on, tell me what you're experiencing, tell me what you're feeling. Somebody please break through these hypothetical questions and memorized responses!"

People start to burnout when religion doesn't reach down to their daily experience. Theoretical religion just doesn't give us anything that will keep us going spiritually. It doesn't produce joyful fellowship. We can continue our church attendance indefinitely. But, without God in the present tense, spirituality withers away. Religion is reduced to sound opinions. There's nothing going on in our hearts.

Controlling instead of shepherding

One reason people get stuck in a religion of theories and opinions is that it becomes a way of asserting control. They may have a hard time getting a handle on their emotions or expressing them well, but, as we have suggested, they can win arguments. People with very little happening in their hearts need to win arguments; they need to succeed with their minds. That's why they get off on elaborate discussions about very minor issues. That's why someone, for example, can construct a whole thesis on why we should do nothing but mourn in church services.

And some people carry this need to control even farther. They are so empty and needy inside that they are compelled to try to control everyone around them.

One day my pastor, Rob, was reminiscing about the people he'd worked with early in his ministry on the East Coast. And he couldn't get one man out of his head, a minister we'll call Joe.

Joe had come out from Oklahoma to head a church in upper New York State where Rob was to serve as a pastoral intern. At first, in his conservative black suit and kindly demeanor, he presented the picture of a fatherly minister. He could play the piano and organ beautifully. He could also take charge and get things done. This was a self-made man who'd worked his way up in the printing business.

And Joe stood by the pillars of Adventism, remarking to the congregation that he would be glad when this "righteousness by faith fad" blew over and everyone could get back to the good old doctrines. He loved to take people on Bible-marking exercises through one proof text after another.

But gradually it became apparent that this man's life and ministry were dominated by one thing: the need to control. He had to control everything.

Joe seemed to have a need to keep his pastoral associate Rob "in his place." Rob had just come from the seminary. Joe didn't have his MDiv. The head pastor's insecurity came out in little gestures. Once during a church service he asked Rob to go get a book from his car, remarking to the congregation, "That's what interns are for." During another service he told the church that ministers should always wear black suits—and glanced over at Rob, who was wearing a gray one.

Joe kept his wife and daughters busy stuffing envelopes and running errands. They seemed intimidated by the steely look in his eyes.

Joe ran the church like a tight ship and would tolerate no differences of opinion. He once preached an entire sermon on the evils of drinking coffee.

But most disastrously of all, Joe began to systematically destroy the work of his predecessor at the church. The previous pastor had been extremely successful in outreach to the community. He started a vegetarian restaurant and hosted a radio program, which quickly became the most popular local talk show in the city. The church was booming.

This former pastor had also been very good at bringing together various ethnic churches in the area. They'd united around a multiracial church school that was providing quality Christian education. Nothing like this had happened in the area before.

But none of this was Joe's doing. He'd inherited this success—and apparently he couldn't stand it. Joe closed the restaurant. He stopped the radio program. And he began to make racist jokes to his elders about "black monkeys." Suddenly racial boundaries became important. Joe kept pointing out that the white churches were providing most of the money for the school. Why shouldn't they have their own? School board meetings, which had been marked by cordiality, became battlegrounds.

Finally Joe's church pulled out of the multiethnic school. Things went rapidly downhill from there. A vibrant congregation of five hundred dwindled to two hundred.

The church was dying—but Joe was in control. He had to control everything and everyone—including the young wife who came for shepherding and ended up in an affair with him. Eventually Joe had to leave that congregation—but ultimately became a pastor in another city.

Some people desperately need to control others. They are not able to get the love they need in healthy ways. They are unable to build healthy, giving relationships. So they try to make other people admire them or follow them or agree with them or obey them.

Healthy people nurture others. They enjoy seeing other people grow. They enjoy giving other people wings to fly.

Dysfunctional people violate boundaries. They get bent out of shape when someone else doesn't tow the line—their line. It's not OK for another member to have a different opinion about Sabbath observance or the investigative judgment. They have to straighten that person out. They have to sabotage their ministry if this "enemy" is in a position of leadership.

It's not OK if someone sings special music in a sleeveless dress. They have to complain about it to member after member until the singer is appropriately embarrassed and changes her ways.

It's not OK if the church votes to lay down new magenta carpet in the sanctuary when they want blue. They have to embark on a campaign to change this terrible error in hue.

Controllers manipulate others in countless ways. They try to make other people feel guilty in countless ways. They draw lines between enemies and friends in countless ways.

The tragedy is that unhealthy people rise to the top in so many congregations. Smaller churches are more vulnerable, but it happens everywhere. Needy people desperately want to be Sabbath School superintendent or head elder or chairperson of the church board. They are eager for these positions of honor and influence. They desperately need approval; they need affirmation. They can't love and be loved, so they have to control.

Healthier individuals are not compelled to seize these positions. They are not as driven. In fact, people who've had a healthy dose of love and nurture in their background often become rather lackadaisical. No obvious needs push them into the arms of God or into service for the church. They don't mind if someone else teaches the Sabbath School class or organizes Vacation Bible School.

But that leaves a vacuum which the controlling are only too happy to fill. So in church after church we end up with rigid superintendents and bullying head elders and manipulative chairpersons.

These are the squeaky wheels that keep getting greased. These are the righteously indignant people that must always be pacified. Healthy people can be happy with either magenta or blue carpet. Unhealthy people can't. So guess who gets to choose the color? Guess who ends up making all kinds of other decisions?

Healthy people can be flexible. Unhealthy people can't. They are obsessed by how things *should* be. Things have to be a certain way. Sabbath School and church have to proceed in a certain order or it just isn't church. The music they're comfortable with has to be played or it's just not worship. So guess who ends up shaping our church services?

It's a little like having the lunatics in charge of the asylum. But since these unhealthy people usually affirm the right doctrines loud and clear and don't engage in obviously immoral behavior, no one seems to notice.

But this wreaks havoc in churches; it destroys the joy of worship, the joy of fellowship. Controlling people, in fact, can create dysfunctional churches that no healthy person in their right mind would join. That's a big problem. We can affirm the "27 Fundamental Beliefs" with integrity and yet harbor in our congregations a sick interpersonal dynamic that wars against the truth. We can open the doors to the church with splendid evangelistic meetings and yet close the door to fellowship with our unhealthy relationships. And no new member is going to stick around for long, no matter how glorious the truths we present in theory.

Churches do manage to confront people who have affairs or embezzle funds or preach heresy. We recognize that these problems could destroy the moral life of a congregation. But we rarely confront people who are manipulative or controlling. We rarely say: This has to stop. You can't hold a church office and treat people like that.

Isolating instead of expanding

Adventists traditionally have developed unique ways of making the church distinctive and separate from the world. Like many conservative Protestants, we have keyed on avoiding the obvious accessories of the sinful lifestyle: drinking, dancing, smoking, worldly places of amusement. But we've also added whole new categories of separation from the world because of the Sabbath and "health reform." There are all kinds of things other people eat that we don't. There are all kinds of things people do on Saturday that we don't do.

We decline coffee and pot roast. We try to explain to acquaintances why we must take a nap or nature walk on Saturday afternoon rather than go with them to a Dodger game.

We're different. We're separate. We explain ourselves frequently by peculiarities of lifestyle. For years we used an unfortunate King James English word to urge each other to be a "peculiar people" set apart from others (instead of "a people that are his very own" (Titus 2:14)).

So we've created our own religious subculture. We can go to Adventist schools, all the way from kindergarten to a postgraduate degree. We can buy our food at an Adventist health store. We can receive treatment at an Adventist hospital. Many of us work in Adventist institutions.

Adventists tend to want to have their own version of everything. Recently, Christian women's magazines have begun to flourish. So we began to publish an Adventist women's magazine. And then there's the Promise Keepers phenomenon. Looking on at this movement, it never occurs to us to simply participate in the spiritual dynamic of Christian men coming together from all backgrounds to commit themselves to be good fathers and husbands. No, we think we'd better create some kind of Adventist men's movement, something on our own—that we can carry out during retreats at Adventist summer camps, where we can peruse Adventist men's books and swap stories about academy and ingathering while eating good Adventist food.

The Adventist Church is powered by its many institutions. And that's a strength. That's probably a major reason why we've been able to maintain our distinctive religious culture. But again, a strength can eventually become a weakness. Institutions can become so successful and pervasive that they isolate individuals from their mission in the world. In fact, people who've grown up in Adventist schools often have a hard time relating to "non-Adventists." We've carved out a social niche for ourselves where our unique lifestyle is comfortable.

But we don't relate to "outsiders" very comfortably.

We have evangelistic relationships. We can be nice to neighbors, putting in a good word here and there, hoping that someday they'll come "into the truth." But we aren't so good at friendships, at dialogue, at understanding people with different values.

To put it simply, we're insecure in the world. We don't wander too far from the shadow of our institutions. Our lifestyle doesn't hold up well out there in a "non-Adventist environment."

As a sophomore and junior at Western Illinois University, I began to work with a dynamic group of students in Campus Crusade for Christ. The experience changed my life. During each Sabbath of those two years, I accompanied my parents to the small Adventist church in a neighboring town. It's difficult to describe the contrast I felt between that congregation and what I was experiencing at Western. On Sabbath mornings, a few elderly souls warbled a couple of humble hymns, accompanied by a whining organ, and went through the same routine—the prayer, the announcements, the offering—that had been going on for decades. Then they settled down to listen to a sermon that reviewed the distinctive virtues of Adventism.

I didn't really blame the members for being old. They couldn't help that. I didn't blame them for leading unexciting lives. These sturdy Illinois farmers with their weathered faces had endured too many harsh winters for mere excitement.

What I couldn't stand was the pride of their isolation. They were isolated from the spiritual revolution taking place just a few miles away on a university campus, isolated from its energy, isolated from its spirit. But instead of admiration, they felt superiority.

These folk in Campus Crusade, they maintained, were just dabbling in the rudiments of the faith. Accept Jesus; that's all they know. But Adventists have so much more light. We can take people so far beyond these elementary things.

This looking-down-our-noses attitude was reinforced by the pastor. He was a kindly man who probably feared Campus Crusade might sweep me away from my Adventist roots. So when we talked, he emphasized the vast amount of new religious truth brought into the world by Ellen White, the prophet of the church.

But in my mind I was screaming, "Why didn't anyone teach me these basics of the Christian life? With all the doctrinal light we've got, why do we know so little about real discipleship?" The people in Campus Crusade seemed a couple of light years ahead of the believers huddled in their pews at the

Adventist church. They may have only had "a little light," but they were sure using it to great effect.

During my two years at WIU, I began to see two different kinds of churches, each one headed in an opposite direction. The kids at Campus Crusade for Christ seemed to be reaching out to all the world with the gospel. The local Adventist congregation was a fortress against the world. It didn't see itself that way. In fact, that little church tried to be a light in the community. Members could be persuaded on occasion to pass out "literature" or invite neighbors to an evangelistic meeting. But in their hearts they were always having to defend "the truth" against the overwhelming pressure of the world. They were a little island in a sea of worldliness, hanging on to twenty-seven distinctive beliefs for dear life. And that strain didn't generate a great amount of joy.

Unhealthy religion requires isolation. It cannot survive out there in the world. It needs a subculture to nurture it. Healthy religion reaches out. Unhealthy religion is defensive; it majors in the dangers of "outside influences."

It's all a question of momentum. Are we extending grace outward or collapsing inward? Which force is prevailing? Of course the church is always going to serve as a refuge to some extent. There are times when we all need to "retreat" from the world and get our bearings again.

But is that what dominates? Is our fellowship dynamic? Does it welcome new people in? Or is it static, built around preservation?

> Discussions that remain on an abstract level.
> Churches controlled by negative and needy individuals.
> Isolation within a subculture.

These are some of the key factors that negatively affect the quality of our worship services; they create our overall experience of church just as much as our twenty-seven fundamental beliefs do; perhaps more so. They are the key reasons so many people are burning out on "doing church."

In the following chapters we'll be looking at specific ways we can create a healthier church experience, something that builds people up instead of burns them out. We'll be looking at what makes worship and fellowship essentially joyful.

CHAPTER
NINE

Becoming Transparent

How do you create the kind of fellowship that builds people up? How do you do it in churches that traditionally have majored in abstract truths and loyalty to religious concepts? What can we do to avoid turning a strength—concern for biblical truth—into a weakness, an exclusively left-brained fellowship?

Some people might conclude that in order to put more heart in our religion, we have to start rolling down the aisles and screeching out our praises like old-style Pentecostals. Some might attempt to turn Sabbath School classes into touchy-feely exercises in pop psychology.

But I don't think God asks us to become something we're not. He doesn't demand that reserved individuals suddenly become emotional. He doesn't ask us to manufacture the right feelings. He simply asks us to start expressing the ones we have. It's called being honest, being transparent.

Alcoholics Anonymous began the day William Wilson called up a stranger, Dr. Robert Smith, from his hotel in Akron, Ohio. Traveling on a business trip, Wilson had felt a strong urge to drink. Though a dramatic encounter with God had given him the upper hand in his long battle with the bottle, he was still tempted on occasion. So he thumbed through the phone book, called up a church, and asked the minister if he knew of any hopeless drunk he could talk to. The perplexed clergyman referred him to Dr. Smith, a desperate alcoholic who'd been unable to stop drinking.

The two men talked for hours. Neither preached to the other. Mr. Wilson simply told his story quietly, and the urge to take that one drink passed. He'd acquired a partner in his lonely struggle, and that sympathetic presence saw him through his moment of great peril.

That's how AA was born—a movement in which equally vulnerable people keep each other afloat—with amazing success. Out of their collective, sinking wills and a decision to rely on God or a Higher Power, stability and resilience are somehow created. A man will tell of sitting for hours in an all-night cafe, filling a notebook with the sentence: "God help me make it through the next five minutes." He calls up an AA member at 4:00 a.m. and soon finds strength in the understanding face of a stranger.

That's what fellowship was meant to be. Just the presence of another believing, struggling person is often enough to nudge us out of our rut or dispel our doldrums. There they are in the flesh, a part of Christ, standing with us. Praise God for brothers and sisters.

These are the people we need to start becoming more transparent with in our Adventist churches. We desperately need to experience fellowship—the real thing. When we just sit there and nod in agreement to the same beliefs and come to a nice conclusion after an abstract discussion, we haven't created any fellowship. No one is edified. No one is built up in Christ. To create fellowship we have to start opening up our hearts to each other. There's no other way.

You can start with Sabbath School. What I hear over and over is this: "I'm afraid to open up in church. I'm afraid of what people might think or say." Everyone wants to fit into the niceness. No one wants to talk about their ugly problems when everyone else is commenting on these lovely Christian concepts. No one wants to be first.

But someone had better break open the death-grip of our endless, sterile discussions. Someone had better talk about right here, right now—this is what's happening, this is what I'm feeling. Someone had better be real and transparent, or our whole left-brained religion may just collapse in on itself.

When Jesus presented himself to a crowd by the Sea of Galilee as the Bread of Life, they were not listening with their hearts. These religious people had been trained for generations in how to dissect the Law with their heads. The leaders among them had devoted their lives to "the truth." But they didn't recognize the Truth in flesh and blood. And when Jesus talked about giving up His flesh and blood as a sacrifice, they balked. Something so visceral, something so powerful just couldn't register as an abstract concept. "How can this Man give us His flesh to eat?"

And most of them turned Jesus off. They would go on having their fascinating discussions until their nation and religion and temple collapsed around their ears.

Nicodemus came late one evening for a polite discussion. He could have debated the issue of Messiahship all night. But Jesus burrowed into his heart with the truth: You must be born again.

The woman at the well wanted to deflect Christ's gaze into her many failed relationships by raising a theoretical question: Which is the real, God-ordained place of worship, Samaria or Jerusalem?

But Jesus zeroed in on her need for the water of life.

Jesus spent much of His ministry trying to get His disciples to listen with their hearts. These men were fairly bright. They didn't assume Christ's warning about the leaven of the Pharisees was aimed at bread-making because they were ignorant. They were just accustomed to thinking in a different way. Spiritual thoughts, spiritual instincts take hold slowly in our spirits.

We desperately need to become transparent before God and before each other. We can't be nurtured any other way. We can't be built up on head knowledge alone. We need to have the eyes of our hearts enlightened.

Here's how you can begin the process:

Start with one person

Sometimes it may seem that there's too much inertia in a congregation. You just can't get everybody to open up when they've been sitting safely in the pews behind their correct opinions for so many years. And often you don't feel safe unburdening your real feelings and problems in front of a church group.

But it's terribly important to somehow get the ball rolling. So you can always start with one person. Find one individual you can trust. Fellowship begins where two or more are gathered together in Christ's name.

I'll always remember Scott Sweet. He understood. This gangly, bespectacled fellow missionary who laughed from deep in his throat and studied the Word with great care could smile empathetically when I talked about my struggles with youthful lust or mentioned the threat of some porn display in a neighborhood store. And I knew exactly what he meant by that pull of the flesh that can turn all our brave stands to dust. He acknowledged the bitter taste of defeat. But most importantly, he resonated with that passion to be pure, something those who've struggled long against a persistent habit sense most urgently.

In our moments of fellowship there was an excitement between us. We weren't just discussing theory. We were talking about our lives. I still vividly recall his New England voice, his wild gestures, and sympathetic eyes as we shared war stories on the stairs between our apartments. I still can hear the album we listened to: "Saved," Bob Dylan's experiment in fundamentalist folk rock. We both reverberated with this raucous, dead-earnest call to persevere: You're gonna serve the devil or serve the Lord.

I remember everything because our spiritual lives turned real then, our souls-in-progress passed back and forth as spontaneously and accessibly as Polaroid snapshots. This sharing proved synergistic. We pushed each other to nobler effort, without pointedly trying. In talking about our very common struggle we produced momentum, a third force more than the sum of our two parts.

Talk about now

The one thing that seems to divide dynamic fellowship from the formal kind is simply the present tense. Real sharing is about what's happening right now. It's not just about what happened in the past. You don't just talk about old sins or old victories. You don't just talk about future expectations. You talk about what's going on in your life right now. Where are you at spiritually at this moment? What are you experiencing? What are you feeling?

Real fellowship brings God into the present tense. That's the bottom line. He's active. He's here.

I'll also always remember my fellow teachers at the Osaka SDA English School in Japan. While working there I got tired of greeting the other teachers with the same old banalities every day. As we passed in the hallway, retrieved our lessons from the lounge, or chatted between classes, our conversation was pleasant enough but not too spiritually exciting. It seemed ironic. Here we were in this utterly secular society trying to present the gospel through our Bible classes and evangelistic meetings, trying hard to help our Japanese friends see the light—and yet that light never seemed to flicker between us. If the gospel was indeed as we presented it, the great Answer for humanity, why did it raise so few echoes in our daily life?

So I got together with a few buddies, and we decided to replace our hey-howya-doin', OK-nice-day routine with one simple question, "What did you learn today?" Many of us were trying to develop a consistent time of devotions each day, spurred on by the task of making Christianity real to people who drew a blank when the word *God* was mentioned. What if we tried to share something specific we'd discovered through our time in prayer and the Word? A few of us determined to ask the question in the morning as our greeting and wait for an answer.

Soon everyone was joining in. The fact that we were asking each other about "right now" helped a lot of us dig more purposively in the Word for something definite to share. And talking about some useful principle reinforced that truth in our minds. We were all helping each other grow; we were all encouraging each other. That ethereal, pious word *fellowship* took on flesh and blood.

A couple of slides, taken in good humor, enshrined our practice. My favorite shows Wendel against a big sun-drenched window; he's pointing to an illuminating text in his open Bible. Facing him, Jeff listens enraptured with arms spread wide, washed out by the light. We had some good laughs—and changed our world. The teacher's lounge and hallways of our English school were never quite the same again.

Learn encouragement

One of the greatest miracles of the New Testament is documented in the first chapters of each of the apostle Paul's epistles. When we speak of Saul the persecutor's conversion, we usually refer to that blinding light on the road to Damascus and his sudden change of allegiance from Jewish tradition to Christ.

But I don't think that's quite the heart of the matter. Many people have radically altered their philosophy of life—apparently without divine assistance. Flaming Communists become fiery capitalists. Pushy apple-pie-and-the-flag apologists become loud-mouthed feminists. Obnoxious John Birchers become offensive Moonies. A change in ideology doesn't necessarily mean something extraordinary has happened.

So, in Paul's case, it could be asserted that an intolerant man simply found a new way to express his fanaticism. I used to fear that this assertion might contain a great deal of truth. Then I decided to study "encouragement" in the New Testament. I wanted to find examples of how the writers of Scripture encouraged their readers. That topical study opened my eyes to the heart of Paul the apostle.

I found myself writing down page after page of wonderfully encouraging texts—all from the epistles of Paul. The man had a marvelous gift for expressing love and faith in people. He tells Roman converts he is convinced they are "full of goodness, complete in knowledge." He tells the Thessalonians of "all the joy we have in the presence of our God because of you." He tells the Ephesians he cannot stop giving thanks to God for their faith and love.

I was deeply moved by the extent of this man's involvement in the lives of others. To Corinthian believers plagued by court disputes, immorality, and even incest, Paul cries out, "You are in our hearts to die together and to live together." Chained to a dungeon wall, he exclaims to the Philippians: "Rejoice in the Lord always; again I will say, rejoice!"

Paul begins almost every one of his letters with a flood of encouragement. His run-on sentences are bursting with good news for people he so obviously loves. These words of grace are even more impressive when we remember they come from a late Grand Inquisitor, the hard-nosed legalist. Now we're at the heart of the matter. Now we see how much really happened after Paul's dramatic encounter on the road to Damascus. This was one fanatic who came in out of the cold.

Toward the end of his ministry, Paul is saying farewell to a group of believers in the port city of Miletus. They gather close about him on the dock as he reminds them of their life together: "Night and day for a period of three years I did not cease to admonish each one with tears." The apostle gives a final message of encouragement, and then the small group kneels to pray. They rise to their feet, look for the last time into the eyes of their father in Christ, and emotions break. Weeping loudly, the believers embrace Paul and kiss him repeatedly. It is a difficult parting.

Paul moves off toward the ship, his friends follow, clinging to him, "grieving especially . . . that they should see his face no more."

I find this one of the most remarkable scenes in Scripture. I doubt any "Pharisee of Pharisees" could have inspired such devotion. Saul the law expert would not have had such a wealth of affection at the end of his career. It was definitely someone else there on the dock tearfully embracing his children in the faith.

Paul had become a great encourager. We see that in the beginning of each of his letters. He didn't just admonish believers to build each other up; he did it very eloquently himself.

Paul shows us that the essence of real fellowship is encouragement, making other people feel good about their faith, making discouraged people feel hopeful, making committed people feel even more devotion for Christ. Encouragement is a powerful weapon against burnout.

Recently our church has developed excellent "relational Bible study" resources that are designed to develop just this kind of sharing among members. There are a wealth of materials available that can help us move beyond debating points to building each other up. It can happen. It can happen in your congregation. I have found that the gift of encouragement can be nurtured in the most unlikely places.

One Sabbath day I listened groggily as our pastor rhapsodized at great length about the value of small-group interaction. He kept commending this kind of fellowship to our white, suburban, comfortable congregation and I, slouching in a back pew, kept retorting privately, "Yeah, yeah, more words. Where's the action? Why don't you just *do it*?"

A week later, the pastor unveiled his plan for starting small groups within the church and invited all to join one. I had to eat my retort; I also had to join a group.

It consisted of several people my age who met each Wednesday evening in someone's home. The pastor led us through exercises in sharing ourselves and building up each other. During the next several weeks I watched us ordinary, unexciting church members become a body of Christ, a living organism. It was amazing what came out of these people I had greeted every week for years with the usual clichés.

And it was remarkable how easily we were able to express genuine love and encouragement once we had committed ourselves to the group. It brought to mind the old college days with Campus Crusade for Christ when I'd felt so spiritually alive. I never thought that experience could be repeated. But there we were on those deep sofas—middle-aged bellies, worries-about-the-kids, mortgages, bank accounts and all—finding out what it meant again to share real life in Christ with one another.

CHAPTER
TEN

Setting People Free

When my friend and pastor Rob told me about the minister named Joe who had such a terrible need to control everything in his church, he also told me about another man he'd met early on in his ministry, a man named James. Decades later, these two individuals still stand out in his mind in striking contrast.

James was a salesman by profession who came from North Carolina. To get a little extra cash, he worked as a janitor in one of Rob's first churches in the suburbs of Washington, D.C. He needed the money to take care of his wife, who'd become an invalid after receiving a toxic dose of the wrong medicine. Also, because of osteoporosis, the woman could break a bone just laughing.

James had more than his share of heartache. And yet people loved to be around him. He seemed like everyone's father in the church and would often give until it hurt him. When a blind man began attending services, it was James who began taking food to him each week and caring for his seeing-eye dog. Everybody came to him with their problems—including Rob. It was a time when Rob was just learning how to pastor a church on his own and James could always be counted on for support and for confidentiality.

This man hadn't grown bitter over the tragedies in his life. He didn't complain about the old cars he had to drive or the fact that he had to mop the floors of the church in the evenings—in spite of his accomplishments in life. Instead, he talked about faith in Christ. What mattered to James was love: the love of Jesus and showing love to others.

Eventually James became the head elder and lay pastor of this congregation. And the church blossomed under his care. Members became more Christ-centered, because James was Christ-centered. They began to care about each other more, because James cared about them so deeply.

James impacted the whole character of that church. But he never tried to control anyone. It just happened. It happened because of small things—a gesture of concern here and there, a tear shed here and there as he prayed open-heartedly about the grace of His Saviour.

James's congregation shows us what can happen when our fellowship is molded not by people who need to hold some church office but by people who are instinctively gracious. In order to create an atmosphere of joyful worship in our churches, we have to enable people like James to become leaders. And we need to break the dysfunctional cycles that keep so many congregations trapped in the control of negative and needy people.

Here's how to take steps toward freedom:

Confront controllers

It may seem very difficult to deal with controlling individuals in important positions. Confronting them can bring on war in the church. Unhealthy people will sometimes do everything they can to hang onto their position. But what we don't recognize is that they are already creating psychological havoc in the church. They are already dooming a congregation to stagnation or decay.

Gloria had served as the Bellmont church representative on the local church school board for seven years. She'd done a good job, but the nominating committee decided it was time for a change; they felt they ought to give someone else a chance. Pastor Jason, of Bellmont, was not prepared for what happened next. Gloria managed to find out that her name wasn't on the new list of church officers. She called Pastor Jason and wailed about how hurt and angry she was about this "totally unfair" treatment. She just couldn't handle the humiliation.

Gloria's lawyer husband Stan started making phone calls. He found out who had first suggested that a new person be nominated and began a campaign to discredit this individual. He tried to bully the pastor into talking the nominating committee into backing down. When that didn't work, he tried to make a deal in exchange for the school board position.

Gloria and Stan began bad-mouthing the members of the committee, saying they were out to get them. They criticized Pastor Jason as spineless. They even sent their seven-year-old boy to a church meeting to ask, with tears in his eyes, why they were kicking his mother out of her office. Stan threatened legal action.

Pastor Jason and his wife had considered this couple their best friends. But now they became their worst enemies. The loss of this precious position had poisoned their relationship, and Gloria and Stan stopped coming to church.

In the aftermath, however, Pastor Jason discovered something very interesting. His church did much better after this high-profile couple left. He hadn't realized how much they'd terrorized the congregation with their neediness and manipulation.

Some engage in serving others because they have to be needed. They don't develop healthy relationships with equals—they create paternalistic relationships. They need others to be dependent. They are traumatized when they can't hold onto certain positions or certain "turf" in the church. The most loving thing a church can do is confront these individuals about their problem. It's *not* helpful to simply enable them to dig into their turf. They need to be confronted—privately, directly, and compassionately—according to the principles Jesus laid down in Matthew 18:15-17.

Motives make all the difference. We can do a lot of right things for very sick reasons. Sometimes people whose own lives are in chaos love to counsel others. They can keep from facing their own issues by facing everyone else's. Needy people love to take helpless individuals under their wing—and keep them helpless and dependent. That gives them a sense of security.

Healthy people serve others because they enjoy doing it. They like people. They make other people more independent. They help develop other people's gifts.

We have to start building the right kind of churches by starting with the right kind of relationships. We can't sit back anymore and just let the needy and the controlling speak and act for the church. We need to have healthy, as well as doctrinally sound, individuals in charge. We need people like James in charge.

Help people blossom

One thing that will help the Jameses in our church rise to the top is a focus on spiritual gifts. We are beginning to recognize that congregations work best when people are encouraged to minister in ways that express their individual gifts. Our particular spiritual gift is what motivates us most deeply. It impels us toward a certain kind of ministry. It also determines the way in which we carry out that ministry.

The Adventist Church Resource Center has developed training materials that an entire church can use to help members discover their spiritual gifts and find the best ways of expressing those gifts in ministry. It's not just a matter of sticking people into roles. It's not just a matter of filling offices in the church. It's a matter of helping people blossom.

That's what's exciting about spiritual gifts. Everyone has something unique to contribute. Everyone has a God-given talent that can be nurtured and developed. Church should be a place where individuals find the freedom to be all they can be in Jesus Christ. Church should be a place where relationships are based on grace, not position, where people seek to multiply giftedness, not protect their turf.

That's why Paul urges us in 1 Corinthians 12 to create spiritual unity on the basis of our diverse gifts. We all need each other in the body of Christ. The eye can't pretend that the hand doesn't belong to the body because it can't see. What would the body be without a sense of touch? And the foot can't be made to feel inferior because it's not an arm or a mouth. How would we ever walk without it?

An awareness of spiritual gifts helps us to honor each other. We learn to appreciate those gifts and talents that may not seem so flashy at first glance. We learn that the person back in the kitchen helping set up the tables for potluck is every bit as much a minister of God as the person speaking at the pulpit. The gift of service isn't some lesser subset of the gift of teaching or preaching. It's a gift from God, period.

An awareness of our diverse gifts in the body of Christ helps us move away from competing for certain positions in the church. It helps us move beyond making others subservient in some way. It moves us beyond a religion of power to a religion of empowering others.

George Vandeman is one of the most driven people I have ever known. You need to have drive to build a television ministry from scratch. You have to have vision. You have to believe that God is going to use you to reach the masses in the great metropolitan areas of the world—and "finish the work."

George Vandeman created the *It Is Written* telecast. It's his baby. It started the year his last child, Connie, was born and has grown up with her.

A man like that doesn't let go of the reigns easily. I became aware of that when I started working as his scriptwriter in 1984. He was still going strong. George enjoyed the benefits of a healthy Adventist lifestyle. And he still had a gift for connecting with viewers in their living rooms on an emotional level. But as he kept going several years past retirement age, the staff began to wonder if he would ever be able to step out of the spotlight.

We needed to find a successor if the telecast was to continue. We tried a few candidates, but some among the staff felt that George was postponing this inevitable step. Perhaps the act of naming a new speaker would be a betrayal in his mind, a betrayal of his belief that Jesus would come soon.

Finally, however, Mark Finley was chosen as *It Is Written*'s new speaker/ director. I was fortunate enough to continue working for the telecast and producing scripts for Mark.

During the transitional period, as Mark was phased in to the telecasts and George was phased out, several staff members still expressed doubts that George would really allow Mark to take control. He'd been in charge so long. He'd always been a very hands-on manager, keeping tabs on every detail—from the color of direct mail pieces to the dinner menus at Partnership fund-raising events.

A lot of people at the Adventist Media Center thought Mark would have to work under George's shadow for some time. It's just human nature. How do you ever really let go of your baby?

I will never forget the day George dropped by the video truck during Mark's first full taping session as *It Is Written*'s speaker. My job is to sit in the control room with my script in hand, facing a wall of color monitors, and make unpleasant noises when the speaker trips up or strays too far from the script. Sometimes the producer even listens to me.

George came in to the darkened room just as Mark was finishing up a strong story and moving in to an appeal for viewers to accept Christ into their lives. George leaned against a soundproof wall, out of the way of the technicians. But I couldn't get my eyes off his face.

The man seemed transfixed. He began beaming as Mark made his appeal. He leaned forward, eagerly nodding. At one point I caught George thrusting out his hands as Mark made a powerful point. It was an involuntary gesture that seemed to be trying to pour even more passion into his successor's body.

Finally I stood up, walked up to George, and put an arm around him. There were tears in his eyes as Mark spoke before the cameras of the grace of Christ. Tears flowed down George's cheeks as Mark led viewers into a prayer of commitment.

Then George turned to me and, slamming a fist into his palm, whispered excitedly, "He's got it! Thank God, he's got it!"

No one else noticed this little exchange in that black room full of glowing lights and screens. No one else heard George's words. It wasn't a speech. It wasn't something for the telecast audience. It was something that came from deep in his soul.

I had become quite fond of George during the years I worked with him. This Christian gentleman was a bit like a father to me. And I admired his calling as an evangelist. But he never stood taller in my eyes than during that moment in the video truck. I don't expect to see in my lifetime a more moving demonstration of John the Baptist's statement about Christ, "He must increase and I must decrease."

Healthy religion builds people up—and then lets go.

Make church safe for creative expression

It's important to understand that along with a variety of spiritual gifts and talents and ministries comes a variety of ways of expressing our faith. Different personalities praise God most genuinely in different ways. Different generations praise God most genuinely in different ways.

So no one style of worship should be imposed on everyone as morally correct. That makes church services stifling. Worship turns into ritual. Everything begins to seem memorized.

The most joyful worship happens when people find a language that speaks to their innermost emotions, that gives voice to their inner self before God. That language could be a certain style of music, it could be a certain kind of congregational sharing, it could be a certain experience that a speaker shares. What will help people find their worship language is to allow room in the church for a variety of creative expression.

Obviously, negative people shouldn't determine the kind of worship that takes place in the Seventh-day Adventist Church. But no one kind of people should. We've got to stop demonizing things we're not comfortable with. The thing that annoys us may be just the language someone else needs to hear. Sometimes we may need to create more than one kind of worship service in a church to meet different needs.

But through all this, it's important to remember that the diversity of members in the body of Christ is something that reflects the breadth of God's character and personality. The diversity of tastes doesn't have to become a battleground. It can remind us that God is bigger than anything we can express, that no church on earth can contain His wonder and mystery.

But our efforts to find a genuine language of praise can help fill out the picture. The variety of our expression makes the tapestry of praise more colorful. High church Bach has something beautiful to say about God. Tranquility and solemnity are experiences that give us glimpses into the unchanging Rock of Ages. Contemporary Christian music also has something beautiful to say about God. Energy and excitement are experiences that tell us something about the God of boundless power who makes all things new.

Something big happened in my heart at the Thousand Oaks Seventh-day Adventist Church several years ago during our Thanksgiving Day worship service. That day is probably meaningful in part because it's something I helped create. I was involved, not just a spectator in the pew.

The service started out with a skit called "Counting to Ten," which I'd written. Three people come into the waiting room of a psychiatrist's office. A neurotic businesswoman, a depressed recluse, and a psychotic. (I played the part of the psychotic; friends assured me, of course, that no acting on my part was required.) The three get into an argument about their respective afflictions; each wants theirs to be the most tragic.

Then the cleaning lady comes in, a simple, elderly woman humming the chorus "Count Your Blessings." She starts chatting with the patients absent-mindedly as she dusts, and eventually their grim introspection is detoured. They begin to ponder things they have to be thankful for—even the psychotic young man manages to do this in his own eccentric way.

In the end, the three patients follow the cleaning lady out the door, intent on seeing if they can count to ten, if they can find that many blessings in their lives.

The skit had a bit of humor, and it opened the congregation's minds to the therapeutic potential of thanksgiving.

Next, three people stood up and talked about a specific incident during the year that had shown them God's providential care. Some had something to share that related to the congregation. Lisa talked about how fellow believers had rallied around her during her surgery for breast cancer. She'd been overwhelmed by the flood of support—all those flowers in her hospital room, the friendly faces dropping by. Lisa and her husband had to move to another house right after she got out of the hospital. All kinds of people had showed up to help load the furniture. People brought lots of food. They even brought their buckets and sponges to make the new home spotless.

Lisa also recalled the elderly woman in church who had told her one day after Sabbath School, "I wish that I could have the disease instead of you." And Lisa realized something amazing as she looked into this fellow church member's eyes: this woman really meant it.

You could tell that the congregation had been moved and warmed by this time of sharing. Thanksgiving had become more than a nice abstraction. It had flesh and blood in these voices, these stories. People were ready to give thanks. We had a wonderful time of singing as several lively choruses made our emotions tangible. You could feel a robust spirit of praise welling up in the sanctuary.

Finally, the pastor wrapped up the service with a short talk that made the meaning of thanksgiving clear and called us all to make an offering of our lives to God.

That was a powerful service. It wasn't just a nice routine where all the familiar pieces fall into their pious places. That day every element formed part of a whole. It captivated the congregation. It moved to a climax; we were really expressing something to each other and to God.

As our church kept innovating in worship, I experienced the pure joy of church for the first time in my life. I'd attended Adventist services since childhood—it was the right thing to do. But I'd been bored out of my mind 90 percent of the time. And I could never quite figure out why, if God was the most captivating personality in the Universe, we typically grew drowsy in His presence. Why did church have to numb instead of inspire?

Finally, after forty years, something was happening. We were involving our whole selves, our hearts and minds and souls and all the talent we could muster, in the worship of our God.

It actually hit me on a Saturday night at a theater in Glendale. The church had planned an outing to see "The Music Man" performed. I sat through the first half suitably amused. It's a nice, entertaining play. But then, during intermission, something wonderful hit me: church was better than this, much better.

That very day the music of praise in the sanctuary, contemporary music that spoke my language, the testimonies shared, the message given—it all had captured me. I'd been engaged, mind and heart, in a much deeper way than I was during the play. Church had been a more powerful experience. I couldn't get over it. That was one of the most exciting days of my life.

Some might conclude that I experienced these feelings simply because my church had degenerated into "worldly amusement"; that we were just trying to compete with the world. All I can say is, if something that makes you pour out devotion and praise to God, if something that grips your heart with His presence, is worldly amusement, then worldly amusement must be a wonderful thing. And we need much more of it.

I dream of a day when Adventist worship captivates the people who walk into church. I dream of a day when we can move far beyond the pedantic routine and mediocrity that pervade so many of our services.

I want to see new music created that moves people today in the way that Bach and Handel's music did centuries ago. I want to hear music that rips my heart out. I want to see our finest art push me into new heights of praise. I want to see drama that makes the Christian life and "the things above" as real as blockbusters make violence and sex real. I want to hear people's lives unraveling from the pulpit, not just their theories. I want people to preach who captivate us with a picture of Jesus working in their lives.

It can happen. It can happen, because I believe there's enough joy in Christ to go around. We just need to make something great out of it.

CHAPTER ELEVEN

Widening Your Circle

One of the reasons Jesus kept getting in trouble with the Pharisees and Sadducees is that the wrong kind of people enjoyed His company so much. Early in His ministry the Messiah "reclined at the table" in Matthew's house with a great crowd of tax-gatherers and sinners. The "right kind of people" wondered: Didn't attending a party like that imply approval of all the transgressions these guests had committed and were committing? Wouldn't the real Messiah express His fundamental separation from this willfully "unclean" bunch?

The Pharisees insisted on knowing why Jesus would eat and drink with such people.

Jesus replied that it's the sick, not the healthy, who need a physician.

But the Pharisees thought this a poor excuse. The essence of their religion, the essence of their identity, was to be different from the people "in the world." The practice of ceremonially washing their hands after they accidentally touched something defiled in the marketplace, for example, wasn't just a little detail of the faith. It expressed what holiness was all about for them: physically set apart.

Christ was socially promiscuous in their eyes. He wasn't discerning. Although even these professional critics wouldn't have accused Him of being sexually promiscuous, they definitely thought the Man was undiscriminating in His social contacts. And that was a big threat. The simple act of an allegedly holy man having a pleasant chat with some ne'er-do-well over supper hammered at the fundamentals of Pharisee religion.

And Jesus kept hammering. He asked Himself over for dinner at the house of Zacchaeus, the most notorious tax-collecting cheat in Jericho. Jesus rescued a woman caught in adultery—right from under Pharisee noses. He permitted a prostitute to wash His feet with her tears and dry them with her hair. He touched every Tom, Dick, and Harry who came from who-knows-where for healing from who-knows-what.

The Pharisees grumbled about this all through Christ's ministry in Perea. They wanted to know why the very worst in society seemed drawn the closest to this Pretender. What did that say about Him? Jesus' parables of the lost sheep, lost coin, and prodigal son were all given to explain His social life. He'd become known, in the nicest circles, as "a glutton and a drunkard, a friend of tax collectors and sinners."

Jesus' contacts with such people were, in fact, wonderfully redemptive. After a little time in Christ's presence, Zacchaeus vowed to restore what he'd cheated, the adulteress resolved to sin no more, and the prostitute became a committed disciple. But the Pharisees couldn't get past the fact that these kinds of people *liked* Jesus so much. They loved to be in His company.

The pure heart of Christ was miles removed from the dirty hearts of His frequent companions. Sin hurt His sensibilities in ways that few of us can understand. So why on earth did bad people feel so comfortable around Christ? Why did they feel such love and acceptance?

Because Jesus didn't spend His time wondering what approval His presence at a certain party might imply. He didn't fret over the possibility that silence might imply consent, that if He didn't rebuke misdeeds He was condoning them.

Christ did not "recline at the table" to position Himself in a certain way; he did so to be with people. Many religious individuals get uptight in the presence of the profane and the promiscuous. They worry. Should they leave the room when someone starts using bad words? What should they do if someone tells a dirty joke?

In other words, religious people get very self-conscious. They are focused on their position, their "influence," the statement they are making. It's a burden they're always carrying around, a burden that can lead to burnout.

I grew up assuming that a vast gulf separated me as a Seventh-day Adventist from everyone else in the world, including Christians of other denominations. No one had to explicitly teach me that—everything in my religious environment implicitly taught me that.

However, it wasn't until I arrived on the campus of Western Illinois University that I discovered what church really is.

It was a tough choice for me to make as a sophomore. My parents taught at Western, but I really wanted to go to Andrews University, imagining that I'd have a much better social life there. I thought I'd be lost in the middle of a huge secular institution of higher learning. Still, I just couldn't see making my parents foot the tuition bill at Andrews, so I reluctantly enrolled in classes at WIU.

A few days later I found, to my great surprise, that I'd fallen in with a wonderful group of kids in Campus Crusade for Christ. It probably happened because I became quite fond of a lovely, dark-haired, blue-eyed girl named Michelle. She was very active in Crusade and one day invited me to a weekend Bible camp the Crusaders had been promoting. Suddenly that seemed like a wonderful idea. The fact was, whatever place Michelle occupied seemed to be bathed in light. Wherever Michelle wasn't seemed enshrouded in a kind of outer darkness.

During that weekend, God reached through my infatuated daze and I learned a new way of studying the Bible devotionally through the simple process of observation, interpretation, application. In all my years of learning doctrine in Adventist schools, I had never been given such a useful tool for taking in God's Word. Now it seemed that God had personal things to say to me. I was being instructed individually about my life. So, of course, I got excited. I started writing things down, practical principles that I was actually uncovering in a book that had seemed rather inaccessible before or at least not really speaking my language.

Michelle invited me to "Leadership Training Classes" on Tuesday nights. This was where university students learned how to be disciples. It was pretty basic stuff, but the atmosphere grabbed me right away.

They sang and then had a sharing time. People stood up and talked about what had happened that week. The sessions went something like this: Somebody introduced a smiling friend who'd been a pagan a few days before and now wanted to "check Jesus out." Everyone cheered. Somebody gave God credit for helping them ace a physics test they thought they were going to blow. A guy said he'd called his dad and made a little bit of friendly contact for the first time in five years. More cheers and shouts of "Right on, Tommy baby." A slightly embarrassed girl talked about a weird guy who tried to hit on her with all kinds of lame lines. But she came back with a few lines about Jesus. And he actually listened. It amazed her. He admitted how screwed up his life was. Cheers, applause, and whistles. A guy stood up slowly and said that his roommate, whom he'd been praying for all semester, had received Christ the night before. Thunderous cheers.

People didn't just murmur Amen; they yelled encouragement. People didn't just talk about providence and grace. They showed it happening. No long sermons. Only dispatches from the front lines. There were tears in a few eyes. And it was rowdy at the same time, out of control in an amiable way. I didn't know quite what to think. There was a spirit there that nothing in my background had taught me to call holy. But I'd never felt God so keenly in the present tense.

One February afternoon, I wandered over to visit a guy named Ken who lived just off campus. I liked this senior business major. He could throw a good spiral when we played pick-up football games. And now he wanted me to join his "action group." As we chatted on an old couch in his living room, Ken began telling me how he'd "found the Lord." He recalled his B.C. (before Christ) days, laughing at himself over all the times he'd put his glasses in his pocket before going into bars so he wouldn't notice how ugly the girls he was picking up were.

Ken seemed like a real human being who had latched onto Jesus. I decided to join his action group.

I'd grown up singing "I'll share my faith with others on life's way" and always feared the prospect of having to do so. People were always talking to us about our obligation to witness or claiming that witnessing was just a natural result of loving Jesus. Well, I evidently didn't love Jesus enough.

Ken didn't talk to me about my duty to witness. He took me out and showed me how.

Once or twice a week we'd walk into the bowels of some high-rise dorm on campus and take unwary peers through the "Four Spiritual Laws" booklet. I felt uneasy about accosting strangers in this way and tried to get my mind off my fears by picturing Ken feeling his way along a bar and bumping into someone of the opposite sex.

But soon I realized that this booklet could open up some wonderful conversations. People were searching for what it's all about. They were looking in all kinds of harebrained ways, but at least they were looking. We could talk about heavy stuff, about where we'd come from, about life.

And often, by the time we said "see you around" to some guy in his room, we'd become pretty good buddies. We'd both done a little bit of soul searching. It felt good. It felt like you really *could* make contact in this vast, secular institution, contact that produced some magical friction between the Holy Spirit and a human life.

I became something of a "one-on-one" aficionado. I didn't always get the details of the Four Spiritual Laws right, but I got into people's heads and hearts. My upbringing had given me an instinctive fear of the big, bad world out there. *Those* people spent every free moment drinking themselves into a stupor or having illicit sex.

But now I was getting to know the infinite variety of human beings in that big, bad world. And they had longings and struggles just like me. They even had spiritual aspirations very much like mine.

But most importantly, I felt I was part of a spiritual movement sweeping through the world. People were "coming to Christ" all around us. They stood up in our Campus Crusade gatherings and described the rush of stepping out of an old way of life and into a new one. We had momentum. Action groups would soon multiply into billions. We were going to change the world.

Worldliness didn't intimidate my friends in Crusade. God's activity in the world is what seemed overwhelming. Those students didn't look any different from their peers "in the world." They didn't have a special language. They didn't listen to classical instead of rock. Nothing on the outside distinguished them. But Jesus was rumbling through their lives. He was working in the present tense. They were getting to know Him. They were working out the "elementary things" of the Christian life. And that made all the difference.

My experience in Campus Crusade made me realize that there was a dramatic alternative to church as a fortress against the world. Fellowshiping with such believers became one of the most exciting and joyful experiences of my life. I knew that maintaining my faith didn't mean I had to remain isolated in a religious subculture.

In the Adventist Church, the pendulum has been swinging away from that isolation for some time now. I believe we are becoming more skilled at relating our faith to the world around us. We frequently try to connect specific Adventist beliefs to the specific felt needs of our secular neighbors. (A Sharing Book of the Year like Martin Weber's *Hurt, Healing and Happy Again* is a good example.)

But we still struggle with old habits that inhibit effective outreach. Our congregations still often lack the kind of momentum I experienced in Campus Crusade. How do we build this kind of spiritual momentum into the experience of church? How do we nurture an expansive faith?

It really starts with our attitudes.

Comfortable with my beliefs

I'll always remember the American businessman I ran into in Bangkok.

I'd just spent three weeks in Rome, Paris, and New Delhi with an *It Is Written* video crew shooting a series of programs I'd written. I'd stopped off in Thailand for a few days on the way home. This very talkative businessman joined me on the canal tour of the city and began describing his previous two wild nights. As we glided along on a wide brown river, he informed me that Bangkok had became quite a center of prostitution. In between the tour guide's explanations of this temple and that royal palace, my companion waxed eloquent on the exotic dances he'd beheld and on some of the amazing positions the female body can get into.

I told him a bit about the video project I'd just finished and mentioned, in passing, how much I missed my kids back home.

We talked about a lot of things, or rather, he talked mostly and I listened. And something happened to this man as our canal tour came to an end. He stopped bragging about his sexual exploits. The man grew quiet, almost reflective. And he confessed that he'd just gotten married in London and here he was doing this stuff . . . I got the sense that he envied my life, even though he didn't know that much about it.

After we'd parted as friends, I realized that there had been a violent collision out there on the canals of Bangkok. Promiscuity and prurient excess had collided with conventional family relationships. And amazingly enough, the latter had won hands down! Me mentioning a few things I enjoyed about my eight-year-old girl and ten-year-old boy had quieted all the talk about sexual acrobatics.

It was a telling moment for me, because I'd assumed most of my life that mere purity would always be intimidated by the pleasures of the world, always be defensive. But I found I was quite comfortable talking about the joys in my home. His stories were interesting (up to a point) but I didn't feel it necessary to express my disapproval or point out the sexually transmitted diseases he'd probably picked up the night before. (My silence probably had more to do with jet lag than any wisdom on my part.) I was just myself, and he came to appreciate that. I didn't try to make him confess the error of his ways. He did so just because he got a glimpse—on his own—of something better.

It's something of a paradox, but the more comfortable you are with your own life and beliefs, the more comfortable you are with people who don't share them. If you're insecure, however, about the lifestyle you've adopted (or that has been forced on you) or you're uncertain about your beliefs, then associating with those who disagree makes you uneasy. It's more of a threat.

I noticed this after I transferred from Western Illinois University—and my electrifying experience with Campus Crusade for Christ—to Andrews University. Few Adventist kids there shared my enthusiasm for witnessing. Even the student religious leaders on campus seemed very reluctant. I could tell them about how wonderful communicating your faith on a deep level had been at Western, but it didn't seem to register. They frequently talked about how easy it was to offend people when you bring up the subject of religion.

Well, in fact, I almost never brought up the subject of religion. I talked about what Christ was doing in my life. But the more I spoke with Adventist kids, the more I came to believe that many of them assumed everyone else would be uptight about religion, because *they* were uptight about religion. They assumed people would be uneasy, because *they* were uneasy. They weren't quite sure that their beliefs would sell in the marketplace.

Interested in other people

Jesus Christ is the greatest force for positive change in our world. He is capable of healing individuals who are profoundly broken. He fulfills our deepest longings as human beings. The more we understand this, the more comfortable we can be with the faith He inspires. And that security can move us beyond the self-conscious inhibitions that so many passively religious people exhibit. We don't have to worry about defending ourselves or our church; we can be interested in other people. The closer we get to the magnetic personality of Christ, the more we get out of ourselves and the more we come to share in His wonderful way of getting into other lives.

Jesus focused on the sick and needy in a way that never made them feel He was condescending. He listened to their lives unravel as they broke bread together. He expressed sympathy and understanding. He made them feel there was hope, that there could be a place for them at the Father's table.

Jesus liked people, period. Part of His genius as the Good Shepherd seeking that lost sheep was that individuals could feel convicted in His presence but never awkward.

Healthy religion causes us to like people. Unhealthy religion makes us uptight and self-conscious. But sometimes it's just a matter of developing more social skills. People who are only used to interacting with others in their subculture need to expand their relationships. And you don't do that just by taking a tract to a neighbor. You don't do that by having an agenda in every conversation, carrying around that burden to somehow insert a few words of witness.

You express an interest in other people's lives. You're just interested in people, period. You don't worry about your approval or disapproval. You're not God. You simply ask people questions, when appropriate. You share something about your own life. When you talk about your own problems, they will talk about theirs. Friendship is about give and take.

When I was teaching English at an Adventist language school in Japan, a few other teachers and I shared a fascinating conversation with a young devotee of a Buddhist sect. Most people in Japan are very secular, so this was an unusual encounter. We invited him over to our apartment for lunch to continue the dialogue.

After chatting for a couple of hours, we parted with our respective faiths intact. He couldn't quite buy Jesus as the Way, the Truth, and the Life. We couldn't quite buy making offerings to ancestors. As he walked to the door, the young man thanked us very politely and reached out to shake our hands. One teacher among us, however, declined the offered hand. For him, shaking hands implied agreement. And he couldn't agree with any of this man's religion. So he couldn't shake his hand.

That gesture, or lack thereof, has stuck with me. It speaks of our religious problem with acceptance. Shaking hands can mean all kinds of things: Thanks for coming; it was nice getting to know you; I'm your friend; I affirm your value as a human being. But a certain kind of religious consciousness turns it into a single thing: agreement, approval.

We need more practice in just shaking hands. By our interest in and sympathy with other individuals, we can accept people we don't agree with. We can accept people who are different from us. We can accept people who are bad. Why? Because they are worth getting to know, period. Because they always have value as human beings. Because Christ died for them. And none of this has anything to do with our approval or disapproval of their beliefs or behavior.

Practice just shaking hands. People are interesting. They're worth getting to know. No wonder God so loved the world that He gave His Son.

Confident that God's way is best

My fellow writer, John McClarty, once told me about a most remarkable couple in his New York City congregation. Vincent and Marilyn Gardner carried on a health–screening van ministry in that metropolis. In a sense, they were very traditional Adventists. They dressed conservatively. They were quite health conscious, maintaining a diet of about two percent fat. They believed they were living in the end times. Vincent and Marilyn had a lifestyle that set them apart from almost all New Yorkers.

Yet John recalls them as two of the most approachable people he'd ever known. They stood at the very heart of the church—not because they defended their correctness more vigorously but because everyone loved them and everyone knew they were loved by the Gardners.

And this wasn't an easy congregation to embrace. It had become a refuge for a wild assortment of human beings: a homeless schizophrenic, a four-hundred pound opera singer, a couple of homosexual businessmen who always came to church in fur coats, immigrants from Africa trying to find their place in the Big Apple, the warped adult children of a dysfunctional evangelist, bitter women who'd spent their lives trying to get guys to sleep with them for more than one night.

There were all kinds of things to express disapproval of in this congregation. But Vincent and Marilyn were not occupied by that. In talking and working with them, John discovered that God's unconditional love lay at the center of their faith and their lives. They talked about forgiveness; God had already forgiven the entire world, through Jesus on the cross. We all need that grace. They could never just thank God that their lifestyle was so different from that of the people around them. They felt the need for corporate repentance—like Ezra weeping before the temple for his wayward people. They felt that "we're all in this together; your sin is my sin." For them the church was a place that welcomed everyone—especially people who thought and lived differently.

That sense of acceptance came through when people visited the Gardner's home and "reclined at table" to enjoy a healthy but elegant and tasty supper. This couple always made people feel comfortable. As John put it, "Every day they spoke and lived a solidarity with the broken people of the city."

Vincent and Marilyn were convinced that God's way is best. They were confident of His love in their lives. They were confident that living within that love is the most wonderful thing in the world. That's why they could reach outside their circle so easily. They weren't uptight because they had a secure faith.

Daniel is a good example here. Nobody in the royal court of Babylon gave a rip about Jewish dietary laws. Everyone in that court was intent on turning a group of Hebrews into good subjects of King Nebuchadnezzar. But Daniel still felt confident that His God had the best plan. That's why he initiated the world's first comparative dietary study. He didn't take the chief steward aside apologetically and ask if he would accommodate "my peculiar religious practices." Daniel challenged his handlers to let him and his friends eat kosher food for ten days, while the other candidates for leadership ate from the king's rich fare. He was confident about who would look better after that period of time. Daniel knew that God's way is best. So he was comfortable living that way in an alien environment.

God is hyperactive on this planet. His grace is performing wonders everywhere. His love is opening eyes and hearts everywhere. Do you believe this is the most important fact in our world today? Whether we're basically isolated or basically expansive is determined to a large extent by our confidence in the power of divine love.

Unhealthy religion starts by drawing a circle that excludes "the world." It must continually narrow that circle in order to try to keep an identity intact. Healthy religion starts within the very secure circle of God's love. From that point it can widen its circle of friendship indefinitely.

Summary of Part III

Healthy Religion Rejoices

Generates joyful fellowship

I have great confidence in you; I take great pride in you. I am greatly encouraged; in all our troubles my joy knows no bounds (2 Corinthians 7:4).

I am glad and rejoice with all of you. So you too should be glad and rejoice with me (Philippians 2:17).

Worships enthusiastically

Sing for joy to God our strength; shout aloud to the God of Jacob! Begin the music, strike the tambourine, play the melodious harp and lyre (Psalm 81:1, 2).

Sing to the Lord a new song, for he has done marvelous things (Psalm 98:1).

Brightens life with a positive outlook

"If your eyes are good, your whole body will be full of light" (Matthew 6:22).

Overflows with thanks

Be joyful always; pray continually; give thanks in all circumstances, for this is God's

Unhealthy Religion Suspects

Can't open up

We have spoken freely to you, Corinthians, and opened wide our hearts to you. We are not withholding our affection from you, but you are withholding yours from us (2 Corinthians 6:11, 12).

Suspects exuberant praise

The whole crowd of disciples began joyfully to praise God in loud voices for all the miracles they had seen: . . .

Some of the Pharisees in the crowd said to Jesus, "Teacher, rebuke your disciples!" (Luke 19:37, 39).

Contaminates life with a negative outlook

If your eyes are bad, your whole body will be full of darkness. If then the light within you is darkness, how great is that darkness! (Matthew 6:23).

Gets stuck in sorrow

Godly sorrow brings repentance that leads to salvation and leaves no regret, but worldly sorrow brings death (2 Corinthians 7:10).

will for you in Christ Jesus (1 Thessalonians 5:16-18).

Sing and make music in your heart to the Lord, always giving thanks to God the Father for everything (Ephesians 5:19, 20).

Is adaptable

I have become all things to all men so that by all possible means I might save some (1 Corinthians 9:22).

Remains rigid

"Nobody has ever heard of opening the eyes of a man born blind. If this man were not from God, he could do nothing."

To this [the Pharisees] replied, "You were steeped in sin at birth; how dare you lecture us!" And they threw him out (John 9:32-34).

Healthy Religion Opens Up
Encourages transparency

We have spoken freely to you, Corinthians, and opened wide our hearts to you.... Open wide your hearts also (2 Cor. 6:11, 13).

Unhealthy Religion Suppresses
Conceals problems behind a nice façade

"They dress the wound of my people as though it were not serious. 'Peace, peace,' they say, when there is no peace" (Jeremiah 6:14).

Shares the personal

We were delighted to share with you not only the gospel of God but our lives as well, because you had become so dear to us (1 Thessalonians 2:8).

Plays with facts

Warn them before God against quarreling about words; it is of no value, and only ruins those who listen (2 Timothy 2:14).

But avoid foolish controversies and geneologies and arguments and quarrels about the law, because these are unprofitable and useless (Titus 3:9).

Experiences new life
. . . but love builds up (1 Corinthians 8:1).

. . . but the Spirit gives life (2 Corinthians 3:6).
"Whoever believes in Me, as the Scripture has said, streams of living water will flow from within him" (John 7:38).

Worships in many ways
Praise him with the sounding of the trumpet . . . with the harp and lyre . . . with tambourine and dancing . . . with the strings and flute . . . with resounding cymbals. Let everything that has breath praise the Lord (Psalm 150: 3-6).

I will pray with my spirit, but I will also pray with my mind; I will sing with my spirit, but I will also sing with my mind (1 Cor 14:15).

Healthy Religion Builds Up
Doesn't have to control
Not that we lord it over your faith, but we work with you for your joy, because it is by faith you stand firm (2 Corinthians 1:24).

Leads by nurturing
As apostles of Christ we could have been a burden to you, but we were gentle among you, like a mother caring for her little children (1 Thessalonians 2:6, 7).

Experiences only theories
Knowledge puffs up (1 Corinthians 8:1).

For the letter kills (2 Corinthians 3:6).

. . . always learning but never able to acknowledge the truth (2 Timothy 3:7).

Can't worship from the heart
"These people come near to me with their mouth and honor me with their lips, but their hearts are far from me. Their worship of me is made up only of rules taught by men" (Isaiah 29:13).

Unhealthy Religion Controls
Has to control
They tie up heavy loads and put them on men's shoulders, but they themselves are not willing to lift a finger to move them (Matthew 23:4).

Plays power games
It is true that some preach Christ out of envy and rivalry . . . supposing that they can stir up trouble for me while I am in chains (Philippians 1:15, 17).

Expresses confidence in others

I always pray with joy . . . being confident of this, that he who began a good work in you will carry it on to completion until the day of Christ Jesus (Philippians 1:4, 6).

I myself am convinced, my brothers, that you yourselves are full of goodness, complete in knowledge and competent to instruct one another (Romans 15:14).

Helps others blossom

Fan into flame the gift of God, which is in you (2 Timothy 1:6).

We proclaim [Christ], admonishing and teaching everyone with all wisdom, so that we may present everyone perfect in Christ (Colossians 1:28).

Healthy Religion Welcomes
Draws a wide circle of love

May the Lord make your love increase and overflow for each other and for everyone else, just as ours does for you (1 Thessalonians 3:12).

Above all, love each other deeply, because love covers over a multitude of sins (1 Peter 4:8).

Flatters in order to manipulate

I urge you, brothers, to watch out for those who cause divisions and put obstacles in your way that are contrary to the teaching you have learned. Keep away from them. . . . By smooth talk and flattery they deceive the minds of naive people (Romans 16:17, 18).

Clings to position

"They love the place of honor at banquets and the most important seats in the synagogues; they love to be greeted in the marketplaces and to have men call them 'Rabbi' " (Matthew 23:6, 7).

Unhealthy Religion Isolates
Draws lines to isolate

Then they hurled insults at him and said, "You are this fellow's disciple! We are disciples of Moses!" (John 9:28).

Since there is jealousy and quarreling among you, are you not worldly? . . . For when one says, "I follow Paul," and another, "I follow Apollos," are you not mere men? (1 Corinthians 3:3, 4).

Minimizes outer differences

Here there is no Greek or Jew, circumcised or uncircumcised, barbarian, Scythian, slave or free, but Christ is all, and is in all (Colossians 3:11).

Accept one another, then, just as Christ accepted you, in order to bring praise to God (Romans 15:7).

Delights in people

I thank my God every time I remember you (Philippians 1:3).

I do not say this to condemn you; I have said before that you have such a place in our hearts that we would live or die with you (2 Corinthians 7:3).

Shows confidence that God's way is best

I have learned the secret of being content in any and every situation, whether well fed or hungry, whether living in plenty or in want. I can do everything through him who gives me strength (Philippians 4:12, 13).

Maximizes outward differences

The circumcised believers criticized [Peter] and said, "You went into the house of uncircumcised men and ate with them" (Acts 11:2, 3).

Finds a way to show disapproval

The Pharisees and teachers of the law asked Jesus, "Why don't your disciples live according to the tradition of the elders instead of eating food with 'unclean' hands?" (Mark 7:5).

Judas Iscariot . . . objected, "Why wasn't this perfume sold and the money given to the poor?" (John 12:4).

Isn't confident that God's way is best

Jesus looked at him and loved him. "One thing you lack," he said. "Go, sell everything you have and give to the poor . . ."

At this the man's face fell. He went away sad, because he had great wealth (Mark 10:21, 22).

The Heart:
From Unhealthy to Healthy

CHAPTER TWELVE

Holes in Our Hearts

In the preceding chapters, we've been looking in detail at the differences between healthy and unhealthy religion. We've zeroed in on contrasting ways we can relate to standards, to the truth, and to the church. Some ways lead to burnout, to compulsiveness, and to isolation. Other ways lead to expansive growth, to an opening of the eyes of our hearts, and to genuine fellowship.

Most importantly, we've seen that the dividing line between healthy and unhealthy religion is this matter of love. Love makes all the difference. Without a foundation of love, we inevitably create an unhealthy religion.

This leaves us with a question: are those who didn't receive an adequate amount of love and nurture in childhood doomed to legalism and the perpetual struggle to be right? Or is there a way out? Can those who didn't grow up with the right emotional resources ever acquire those essential tools and build a healthy religious life?

After all, the amount of love we receive from our parents determines to a large extent the amount of self-esteem or security we have growing up. The heart is like a sponge that must soak up a certain amount of emotional nutrition. If you receive a healthy dose of care and nurture as a child, you'll become a healthy, well-adjusted adult. If you receive a minimal dose of care and nurture, you'll most likely become an insecure adult.

At first this seems like a problem with a pretty clear solution. If you didn't receive enough love from your parents, then get it from another source. If your heart is only a quarter full or a half full because of an inadequate amount of love, then surely a spouse, a friend, or God can fill you up the rest of the way.

Unfortunately, it's not that easy. Making up for a lack of love and nurture in childhood proves to be one of the most difficult tasks in all of human life. People twist themselves into all kinds of emotional shapes trying to get enough *in*. When we aren't filled up, something happens to that sponge, to the state of our hearts.

The insecure generally try to get enough inside in one of two ways; they tend toward either passive insecurity or aggressive insecurity. Both of these create the kind of dysfunctional religion we've been examining in the first three sections of the book. But they tend to create opposite styles of dysfunction. It's sometimes useful to understand how these styles contrast with each other.

First, let's look at the aggressively insecure person. We'll call him Tin Soldier Tim; he's always on the march as he tries to get enough *in*.

Tin Soldier Tim fills the emptiness basically by performance. If he's a more secular individual, he tends to be a workaholic. He can never be quite successful enough. And he just has to have the latest, most expensive gadgets, whether he can afford them or not. Other people might shrug off the scratches on their cars with "Oh, well, it runs good." But Tim's got to have a looker. He's always got to have more things, better things.

If Tim is more religious, he is driven by the need to appear more righteous than his neighbor, to have higher standards than his neighbor. How does he do this? He's always on some campaign to change the church or reform other people. He's driven to assert that he's OK by the sins he opposes. Tim has to be right. He violates other people's boundaries. It's not OK if someone else in church enjoys a different style of worship than he does.

In other words, Tim fits the classic profile of a legalist. We've already dealt with several of his key characteristics in previous chapters.

On the opposite end of the emotional spectrum from Tin Soldier Tim stands the passively insecure person. Let's call her Rag Doll Rhoda. Her style of dysfunctional religion doesn't stand out as clearly as Tim's, and so we don't recognize it as often.

Rhoda tries to fill the holes in her sense of self by dependence. She attaches herself to people like a barnacle. Sometimes she tries to live her life through them. Tin Soldier Tim is always on the march; Rag Doll Rhoda is always working on relationships. Tim has to be right. Rhoda has to be needed. That's the warm blanket she's always trying to cling to. She may volunteer for Pathfinders and the social committee and Community Services—just to get intertwined with other people. Often she's entangled in awkward and uncomfortable relationships because she tries too hard.

A certain Greek philosopher managed to get in good with the tyrant Denys and acquired a very comfortable living. He saw another philosopher, Diogenes, cleaning vegetables one day and said, "If you would only learn to flatter King Denys, you would not have to wash lentils."

Diogenes replied: "And if you had only learned to live on lentils, you would not have to flatter King Denys."

Rag Doll Rhoda can't be content with common lentils. She's too empty for that. She's got to get in good with the important people. She has to flatter or ingratiate herself. She has to be needed.

Rhoda always feels, subconsciously, that other people are responsible for her happiness. She's a vacuum cleaner trying to suck up every little shred of approval and affection. And yet nothing sticks. It's never, never enough.

Rhoda is passive, but she manipulates. She tries to control other people by playing the victim. She makes people feel sorry for her. She tries to make them feel responsible for her misery.

Tin Soldier Tim and Rag Doll Rhoda are both desperately trying to put things inside, trying to fill up their hearts—and yet they never get filled. Why? Why is it never enough?

Remember the model of our hearts as a sponge. Something happens to that sponge when it receives only a minimal amount of nurture and caring in the formative stages. It gets hard. It loses its capacity to absorb. Cracks and fissures develop in the sponge. In other words, people develop holes in their hearts.

And so later, even when a spouse or a friend tries to pour love in, that love is not really absorbed. Even when their life is filled with nice things and status symbols, it's never enough. Affirmation doesn't become a part of the person. It seems to go right through them.

This is especially apparent among individuals who were traumatized as children. You feel for them. You want to help them. You try to care for them and express support and affection. But so many times it all seems to go right through. It just doesn't stick. It's not absorbed.

That's the big problem we face as human beings: the shape of our hearts, not being able to absorb the love we desperately need. And this is what lays the groundwork for burnout.

To put it simply: People burn out in the Christian life when what they're putting out is much more than what they're taking in. You have to receive in order to keep giving. When performance (what you're putting out) exceeds nurture (what you're taking in), then you start to run on empty. You can't go on forever with a deficit.

But this brings us to an important question. Can't *God* fill people up who are struggling with emptiness? Can't *God* make up the difference?

God certainly can. Unfortunately, insecure people often put up barriers that keep Him from filling them up.

Tin Soldier Tim, the aggressively insecure individual, typically wields God like a club in order to control other people. He uses God to straighten them out. Tim doesn't take in Bible verses as loving messages from a Father that could fill his heart. Texts of Scripture are weapons he uses to win arguments. He doesn't develop a healthy relationship with God, because he's always trying to manipulate Him.

Rag Doll Rhoda, on the other hand, is always begging God to rescue her. Her life's usually somewhat out of control. God wants her to focus on her deeper needs. But she just wants Him to bail her out of the present mess. She's always keying on superficial, temporary solutions. You hear her saying, "If we just moved into a bigger house, my husband and I wouldn't get on each other's nerves." Or, "If we can just make it through this month, everything will be great."

Rhoda keeps begging God, and she keeps on being disappointed— because her life is still a mess. She won't look at real solutions. She won't look at what God really wants to change. This blocks the development of a healthy, nurturing relationship with Him.

Both Rhoda and Tim throw obstacles in God's way. That's why they're not receiving what they need. But they have to keep putting out—to stay in the church, to be accepted by peers, to feel that they're OK.

Tin Soldier Tim, driven to perform, becomes a *strict legalist*. He tries to be accepted by God by doing the maximum.

Rag Doll Rhoda generally becomes a *loose legalist;* she tries to be accepted by God by doing the minimum. She tells God she's a victim and that since this is all she can put out, surely it must be good enough for Him.

People don't realize you can be a legalist either way. The person congratulating himself because he didn't commit adultery or murder this week can be just as legalistic as the person boasting that he got the victory over ice water or mayonnaise. It's what drives you that matters. Both the *strict legalist* and the *loose legalist* are trying to earn God's acceptance by *doing*, either by doing the maximum or doing the minimum.

Tin Soldier Tim and Rag Doll Rhoda represent two extremes of the emotional spectrum. They are the two tracks that lead most directly to burnout. Most of us fall somewhere in between. And some even fall right in the middle—that is, some individuals come from a very secure background.

But even people who received a healthy dose of love and nurture in childhood can face special spiritual challenges. They tend to develop holes in their hearts of a different kind.

Very secure, self-sufficient people can become what we'll call Laid Back Larry. Larry comes from a warm family. He's not driven to meet urgent emotional needs. So when the good news comes to him—*God loves you!*—he says, "OK, God loves me; of course He does. Now what time does the ballgame start?" Or Laid Back Linda may say, "God loves me. Thanks. What time does Bullocks open?"

God's love often doesn't make much of an impact. Why? Because everybody loves Larry. He's doing fine. His heart is already filled up. And he tends not to have the obvious problems of Rhoda and Tim, so he doesn't feel the need for more. Larry has a bumper sticker that says: "There's too much apathy, but who cares?"

Laid Back Larry has holes in his heart on the exterior. God's love sort of flows around him. He doesn't absorb it.

Tim and Rhoda unwittingly block God's love. Laid Back Larry takes it for granted. It doesn't sink in. Yeah sure, it's been around forever, so what? He doesn't burn out. He sort of browns out, loses interest. That happens to a lot of Christians in middle age. We begin to take God's love and grace for granted.

We all struggle with holes in our heart of various kinds. For that reason, it's very important to understand what we *can't* fix and what we *can* fix in our lives. This is vital.

First of all, you can't fix the past. You can't manipulate other people into making up for what your parents didn't provide for you emotionally. You can't get a big enough house or an important enough position in the church to make up for it. You can't get enough inside that way.

It's like trying to swallow your stomach. It's like trying to market powdered water. What would you add to it?

You just can't fix the past.

You can only fix one thing. You can only work on this one area: your ability to take in the good stuff, *your capacity to absorb love.* You can work on the sponge. You can fill the holes in your heart.

There's only one reason we can hope to do that. God has given us a wonderful promise that summarizes his new covenant with humanity: "I will give you a new heart and put a new spirit in you; I will remove from you your heart of stone and give you a heart of flesh" (Ezekiel 36:26).

God can deal with that heart of stone, that sponge that has grown hard and cracked. He can create in us a heart of flesh, a heart that is capable of absorbing His love and nurture.

If we're willing to allow God to work in this crucial area—our capacity to absorb—then real change is possible. Tin Soldier Tim and Rag Doll Rhoda can escape from their ruts. We have to remember that it's not just what happened to us in the past that keeps us imprisoned. It's not how other people treated us or still treat us. That's not what's messing up our life. It's our inability to absorb the good stuff in the present that keeps us handicapped.

But God offers hope. He wants us to focus on the real solution. The New Testament emphasizes growth on the receiving end, the development of our ability to absorb the good stuff. Here's Paul's great wish for believers: "I pray that out of his glorious riches he may strengthen you with power through his Spirit in your inner being, so that Christ may dwell in your hearts through faith. And I pray that you, being rooted and established in love, may have power . . . to grasp how wide and long and high and deep is the love of Christ, and to know this love that surpasses knowledge—that you may be filled to the measure of all the fullness of God" (Ephesians 3:16-19).

How do you get filled up? How do you get enough *in?* By learning to *grasp* more of the positive (instead of remaining fixated on the negative). By learning to absorb God's love and expand in it. To be filled, you've got to grasp what's available right now.

Here's the apostle Paul praying again for believers: "I keep asking that . . . the glorious Father, may give you the Spirit of wisdom and revelation, so that you may know him better. I pray also that the eyes of your heart may be enlightened in order that you may know the hope to which he has called you, the riches of his glorious inheritance in the saints, and his incomparably great power for us who believe" (Ephesians 1:17, 18, 19).

We need our hearts stretched, the eyes of our heart enlightened, so we can appreciate divine hope, riches, power. The only way we can be filled up is to work on the state of our hearts, on the receiving end.

Many of us have seen, on occasion, glimpses of God's love. We discover some act of divine providence or encounter some particularly gracious Christian. And sometimes this can become a very redemptive experience. A good example is the story related in chapter 4 of how God's love finally became real for a young introverted man named John. But for too many of us these glimpses, these experiences, just don't sink in. The impression fades away. We go back to old habits of the heart.

What we're talking about in these last two chapters is how to grab hold of those providences, those encounters, so that they can sink into our hearts. How do we start building on the good stuff instead of endlessly processing the bad stuff?

One of the first things we need to understand if we are to grow out of our emotional limitations is this: *God is bigger than our hearts.* We can't just remake Him in our own image. We have to stretch to reach around His height and depth, breadth and width.

It's important to stretch, because so often we see only one side of God, the side that's most compatible with our dysfunction. Unhealthy religion always zeroes in on one part of God's character and de-emphasizes something else. The chronically critical promote a God of judgment. Those stuck in a religion of quantity proclaim a God of law, a God who dispenses statutes for every occasion. On the other hand, people whose lives are out of control or who've grown cozy with immorality tend to focus exclusively on a merciful God who would never think of making moral demands on anyone.

We end up with a God closer to our own size and as a result, we never expand beyond our hang-ups. A partial God can never expand us. A partial God can never really fill us up either. He only reinforces what's already there.

We desperately need to see more, to grasp more, to absorb more. We need a bigger God. We badly need to take in more of a bigger God. That's how we work on the receiving end, the state of our hearts.

Let me give you an example of just how much the Almighty encompasses. There are two books in the Bible, especially, that give Rag Doll Rhoda, Tin Soldier Tim, and everyone in between a valuable perspective. Isaiah and Ezekiel present us with starkly contrasting pictures of God.

The book of Ezekiel presents us with a Sovereign God who is looking down on Israel at the end of its long, moral decline. It's an acutely painful spectacle. And one thing dominates in this book. God, the prophet announces, is horrified by sin. In Ezekiel, transgression is never just a misstep, an error in judgment. It's an outrage. God typically thunders: "You have defiled my sanctuary with all your vile images and detestable practices" (5:11). Over and over in this book you hear words like "detestable practices," "lewdness," and "promiscuity." The wicked don't just die; they rot away in their iniquities.

Ezekiel uncovers corruption in high places. In one vision he looks inside the holy temple and sees elders in a cloud of incense, surrounded by carvings of beasts and every creeping thing; they commit abominations in the dark before carved images thinking "The Lord doesn't see us."

In Ezekiel, God is the Sovereign Lord of judgment. The book is scattered with dead bodies and bleached bones. Evil becomes a tangible, graphic image: "I will lay the dead bodies of the Israelites in front of their idols, and I will scatter your bones around your altars" (6:5). And after judgment, after the arrogant and immoral have been crushed, we hear this phrase repeated, "Then you will know that I am the Lord." That's how people are compelled to acknowledge the Sovereign Lord.

This is the picture that stands out in Ezekiel. His God of fierce judgment is not someone most of us instinctively admire. But just wait.

Isaiah gives us another picture. This prophet also includes warnings and proclamations of judgment. But something else dominates in this beautifully written book: the mercy and tenderness of God. Isaiah gives us one image in particular that no other Old Testament prophet expresses: God as a nurturing mother.

Here are some of Isaiah's most moving assurances, given as the Word of the Lord:

> As a mother comforts her child, so will I comfort you (66:13).

> "Can a mother forget the baby at her breast and have no compassion on the child she has born? Though she may forget,
> I will not forget you! See, I have engraved you on the palms of my hands; I covered you with the shadow of my hand. (49:15,16)

Isaiah shows us a God with a tender hand and a tender heart:

> A bruised reed he will not break, and a smoldering wick he will not snuff out (42:3).

This prophet finds eloquent ways to tell us that we are precious and honored in the Lord's sight.

> He tends his flock like a shepherd: He gathers the lambs in his arms and carries them close to his heart; he gently leads those that have young (40:11).

> Even to your old age and gray hairs . . . I have made you and I will carry you; I will sustain you and I will rescue you (46:4).

Isaiah is full of beautiful pictures of a merciful, nurturing God. Both he and Ezekiel present a variety of messages, of course, in a variety of settings. But in Isaiah it's the Suffering Servant, it's tenderness, it's Mother-love that stands out. In Ezekiel, it's the Sovereign Lord of judgment.

Two books give us two contrasting pictures of God. And we can find both of these pictures echoed in other passages throughout the prophets: God as a consuming fire, God as a tender heart.

What do we usually do with those two pictures? Generally we fight over them. We stake out our turf on one side or the other and conduct theological warfare.

Tin Soldier Tim, for example, likes to hurl the God of judgment at poor Rhoda. Her life's a mess; she needs to straighten out. Tim wants to nail her to the wall with a few choice verses about hidden abominations and bleached bones.

Rag Doll Rhoda, on the other hand, keeps trying to fend him off with verses on God's mercy. She needs to be bailed out of yet another predicament. She only wants to look at the God who's an easy touch.

We wage many battles in church over all kinds of issues from these two positions. One side keeps yelling "The law, the law." The other answers with cries of "Grace alone, grace alone." It's mercy versus judgment, forgiveness versus accountability, love versus discipline. And we keep arguing because we need so badly to be right; we need so badly to fill up those holes in our hearts. Doctrinal battles are most fierce when they are least about God.

Both sides can keep lobbing Scripture back and forth because both sides have plenty of vivid images, plenty of explicit texts, to back them up. Both sides have "the truth" on their side.

But they don't have something very important: two pictures. We have two contrasting portraits in the Bible for a reason. God wants us to put them together and begin to see something much bigger than ourselves. He wants to open the eyes of our hearts as we behold the collision of these divine qualities.

It's not enough for us just to say, with Laid Back Larry, "Well, OK, he's a little of both." No, God is a *lot* of both. God is 100 percent a consuming fire of justice. God is 100 percent a tender heart of mercy. He's not 50 percent of each, half just and half merciful.

The Incarnation is a useful model here. Jesus didn't minister in Galilee as half God and half man. He was 100 percent divine, 100 percent human. Only God can create such a combination.

And only God can be completely merciful and completely just at the same time. We can't begin to imagine how passionate He is about justice and righteousness or how deeply He is wounded by sin. But also, we can't begin to fathom how compassionate He is about human frailty.

Human beings can be transformed when both of these pictures come together. Our hearts are stretched when justice and mercy strike simultaneously. Have you ever noticed that this is exactly what happens in dramatic conversions? Read the accounts. You'll often find that, at the moment of conversion, the individual is intensely aware of both justice, the sinfulness of sin, and of mercy, the graciousness of God, simultaneously.

But most of us don't get it. Most of us just settle on our familiar turf and throw texts at the opposite side. Part of our problem with the height and breadth of God is that we just don't know too many people like Him.

We can find straight arrows walking around, people who are zealous for goodness. But they are precisely the ones least likely to understand the weak or show compassion on those who fail morally.

And we have the accepting types, nonjudgmental, easy touches. But they are least likely to give a rip about righteousness.

Most human beings just don't have room enough to reflect both of these contrasting qualities to any significant degree. But once in a great while, we run across someone who brings these opposites together in their lives. These are the individuals who have a tremendous impact on everyone around them.

I think of someone like Corrie ten Boom. The ten Boom family hid Jews in their home in occupied Holland during World War II. This unassuming matron stood for justice when all hell was breaking loose. The Nazis sent her to a concentration camp as a result. But in that camp, thrown in with thieves and prostitutes, she demonstrated great compassion and understanding. All kinds of people wanted to huddle around her when she read quietly from a copy of the Bible she kept hidden near her bunk.

I watched a film made about Corrie that was made shortly before her death. She said the most ordinary things about Jesus being with us and acting as our Victor. They were old phrases I had nodded off to countless times in church. But when she spoke, I almost wept. Familiar words now pierced me to the marrow because I knew who she was and what she had done. There was a breadth to this woman that stretched my heart.

That's the way God is. That's why He moves and inspires so many of us. No one sees more deeply into our moral failings, and no one believes in us so ardently. When He whispers words of mercy, we are warmed by a soul burning for righteousness. When He shouts in fiery judgment, we know that His tender heart is breaking. He is the great encourager, the One who pulls us out of the pit, lifts up our heads, and fulfills all our desires for goodness.

So instead of arguing a certain position and proving ourselves right, let's just for once fall on our faces and say, "God is bigger than what my heart contains. God is better, more just, more merciful than I can imagine."

CHAPTER THIRTEEN

Can You Just Admire?

Jesus and His disciples once stopped off for a brief rest at the home of Mary and Martha in Bethany. Always-on-the-go Martha scurried around getting supper ready. Her sister just sat on the floor listening to Jesus talk. Martha started getting more and more frustrated as she bustled by, sighing and gesturing to let everyone knew how busy she was. Mary wasn't getting the hint. So finally she blurted out to Jesus, "Lord, don't you care that my sister has left me to do the work by myself? Tell her to help me!" *Luke 10:40).

Jesus turned to her and said, "Martha, Martha, . . . you are worried and upset about things, but only one thing is needed" (10:41, 42). These words were addressed to someone not unlike Tin Soldier Tim. Martha was running around performing, trying to make everyone feel bad for not paying more attention to her frantic preparations. But only one thing was really important. And Mary had chosen "what is better." She had chosen something that would not be taken away from her, something she could build on. She had chosen to sit at Jesus' feet and simply *admire*. That's the only thing that's really necessary. And that's something insecure individuals almost never do. Holes in our hearts always push them to blame instead of admire. They blame other people. "They're responsible for my misery; if only so-and-so wasn't such a jerk; if only my mother hadn't . . ."

Tin Soldier Tim is too busy manipulating and controlling to just admire. Rag Doll Rhoda is too busy begging and playing the victim to just admire. Their needs are great. They have all this emotional energy churning inside, but they keep investing it in unhealthy ways.

How are we going to use our emotional energy? What are we going to focus on? That's a choice we have every day. Are we going to invest our energy in blaming other people or in admiring God? If we would invest some time each morning in admiring—meditating on, praying about, and focusing on— what God is like, we will find we have less and less energy to blame and manipulate other people.

That's how we can let God work on the state of our hearts, on our capacity to absorb more. That's how we grasp and stretch and absorb more of a bigger God, a God who is larger than our hearts. It comes down to one word: *admire.* We fill up the holes in our hearts—by admiring. That's how we cooperate with the Holy Spirit in His work of filling us up.

We can start with the quality of our devotional life. When was the last time you spent time in prayer just admiring God?

When Tin Soldier Tim prays, he typically sends God out on errands. He wants God to straighten out those who disagree with him. He wants God to deal with the terrible state of affairs in the church. Rag Doll Rhoda is stuck in her emergency mode, begging for another bail out.

Do you know what one element of personal prayer almost all of us neglect? Praise. Healthy prayer involves petition, intercession, thanksgiving— and praise. Scripture repeatedly refers to the power of praise. And it gives us 150 ways to praise God—just in the psalms. Praise is a means God uses to help us absorb the good stuff. So learn to express back to God what you learn about Him. Don't just make speeches about God's goodness or grace. Talk to Him directly about it. Give voice to your admiration. I have found that nothing has a more immediate, more positive effect on my state of mind and state of heart than a good session of praise with the Father. That's how we admire. That how we start getting filled up.

Share your praises with other people too. Let friends know what you're learning about God. This is yet another reason to move our Sabbath School classes beyond abstract discussion and into sharing about real life. It may help you to find a partner with whom you can share positive experiences. During the day you may pick up small acts of providence, little signs of divine care. Don't let these slip by unacknowledged. Share the good stuff. God's input is all around you. Talking about it with a friend helps you absorb it.

But most of all, we learn to admire through the Word. Studying the Bible isn't enough. It's *how* we absorb Scripture that makes a real difference. Many times, in our reading of the Bible, we do everything except admire. Rag Doll Rhoda is desperately scrounging for promises that will rescue her from some mess. She uses the Bible primarily as first aid. Tin Soldier Tim is always digging up proof texts to argue with, texts that will prove other people wrong. Laid Back Larry is just reading his Bible out of habit, if he does so at all.

We've got to move beyond seeing the Word as essentially a textbook full of doctrinal information. Many of us tend to comb through passages, pulling out texts and phrases and words that support a certain position. The Bible does, as a matter of fact, have a lot of doctrinal information, and objectively analyzing and putting together its data is important. But devotional study is something different; it goes beyond information. And devotional study is the only kind of Bible study that sustains spirituality.

I happen to do a lot of analytical Bible study for various writing projects, and I've done it regularly in the morning. But I've come to realize that it's possible to come away from all my neat categorizing with no more inspiration than from an hour underlining a tome on biology. I need something more to make it devotional. I need the Word to sink into my heart and enlighten me. I need the Word to pierce me like a double-edged sword and get down to my attitudes and emotions, down to the "dividing of soul and spirit."

Mrs. Willencot was a very frugal woman, careful with every penny. When her husband died, she asked a newspaper employee how much it would cost for a death notice.

"Two dollars for five words," he replied.

She asked, "Could I pay for just two words: 'Willencot dead.' "

"No, two dollars is the minimum. You still have three words"

Mrs. Willencot thought a moment. "OK, how about: 'Willencot dead. Cadillac for sale.' "

Obviously, this widow was just counting the words, not expressing a personal grief. She apparently had nothing to express about her husband on an emotional level. His death hadn't sunk in on a emotional level.

Unfortunately, a lot of us are just counting words as we read Scripture, performing a duty or gathering doctrinal information. The question is, do God's nurturing messages really sink in on an emotional level? Do we find something to admire, something we are compelled to express?

How about claiming that spirit of wisdom and revelation that Paul enthusiastically recommends? Ask God to show you something new about Himself in the Word. Make a discovery. Find something new to admire. That's how God starts stretching your heart and helping you grasp more through His Word.

Helen Keller grew up in her own world, shut in by blindness and deafness. She became an almost uncontrollable "wild child" of intense passions. One day while Helen was playing with a new doll, her long-suffering tutor, Anne Sullivan, placed the toy in her lap and signed out "d-o-l-l" in Helen's palm repeatedly. But Helen didn't understand. As the tutor tried to connect this thing in her lap with the signs on her palm, the girl became agitated. She slammed the doll on the floor, breaking it in pieces. "In the still, dark world in which I lived," Helen would write, "there was no strong sentiment or tenderness." She felt no sorrow or regret.

Later Miss Sullivan took the unruly girl down the path to the well house. Someone was pumping water. Placing Helen's hand under the cool flow, the tutor spelled out "water" on her other palm. Suddenly it clicked.

Helen recalled, "The mystery of language was revealed to me. I knew then that 'water' meant the wonderful cool something that was flowing over my hand. That living word awakened my soul, gave it light, hope, joy, set it free!" Now Helen felt eager to learn.

As they returned to the house, she began touching objects.

Each one seemed to quiver with life. And then her fingers touched the broken doll. "My eyes filled with tears," she wrote; "for I realized what I had done, and for the first time I felt repentance and sorrow. . . . That evening . . . for the first time [I] longed for a new day to come." The soul of this wild child, shut away in her own dark world, was wakened by the discovery of the living word.

That's the kind of discovery we need to make. God's Word is not just a store of information waiting to be processed into the right doctrinal categories. It's a way to admire. It's the water of life waiting to fill up our hearts. It's a response to personal revelations. It's having the "eyes of our hearts" enlightened.

The gospels are a great place to start. If you want to get a glimpse of the breadth and height and width of God, all you have to do is take a good look at Jesus' life. He was a wonderful artist of the Spirit who laid out a canvas portraying what God is really like. You get a sense of what a Master He really was by looking at all that He placed on just one canvas. Take a look at just one scene, one afternoon in Jerusalem.

Jesus walked through the covered colonnades surrounding a spring-fed pool called Bethesda and looked out over the human wreckage hovering about it. Pale bodies racked by fatal diseases panted on filthy mats, their faces turned toward the motionless surface of the pool. The blind crouched on the stone porches, their heads cocked, ready to spring toward the first sound of water lapping on stone. The maimed sprawled in a variety of positions, trying to keep their good limbs ready for propulsion. And the most pathetic, those completely paralyzed, lay near the water, staring up at the cold columns, hoping against hope.

These afflicted people were waiting for the miracle. They believed, or tried to believe, that an angel came down from heaven periodically to stir the waters of Bethesda and that the first one into the pool after each disturbance would be healed of his disease. And so they waited each day as the sun rose overhead and fell in its wearying cycle. Some veterans of Bethesda crawled close to the water when they smelled sheep. They imagined that a breeze strong enough to bring them the pungent odors of the Sheep Gate market a few blocks away might be strong enough to help that angel disturb the pool. Others had trained themselves to detect a faint rumbling underground that was usually followed by heated water bubbling to the surface.

Jerusalem was in the midst of a great holy feast, and Jesus had come here to participate as a good Jew in the elaborate rituals of the temple. On this high Sabbath day, He'd gone out from the pomp and pageantry for some fresh air and had been drawn to His more natural environment—the dark corners where the poor and afflicted huddle.

Jesus glanced around at those gray faces dying of suspense, meshed into a crowd where only one could win, and He longed to cause a real disturbance by healing them all. But He knew that such a mighty work during this feast day in a Jerusalem bulging with pilgrims would bring things to a climax too quickly. His ministry would be cut short. Over-enthusiastic crowds had already prevented Him from ministering in certain areas.

Jesus' eye fastened on one particularly hopeless case, one of the paralytics staring up at the columns, and He walked over and started a conversation. Jesus found out that the man had been an invalid for thirty-eight years, enduring a lifetime of physical limbo. Its only interruption in recent months had been a mad rush every few days in which the less disabled trampled over him on their way to the bubbling pool.

Jesus reached down into this bottomless black well of despair and asked a simple question "Do you want to get well?"

It seemed at first like a stupid question. Of course the man wanted to get well. Why else would he expose himself to cold and heat every day amid those stinking colonnades? But, of course, this was Jesus' way of dropping a little hope into the well. It was the first morsel a starving man gets that prepares him for the feast later.

And it was more. Here Jesus presented Himself as servant. He was not the great miracle worker parading through, who condescended to pass His wand over some lucky wretch. He was a servant asking if He could be of help. Jesus' power, always tempered by grace, was never overbearing.

The paralytic could think only of the pool. If just once he could be the first one in. He'd managed to persuade acquaintances to carry him to Bethesda but no one wanted to hang around all day waiting for the water to move. Maybe—just maybe—this kind stranger would give him a push at the right time.

Jesus seized this ray of hope and bent it from superstition to Himself. He looked into the man's eyes and uttered a perfectly ridiculous command: "Get up! Pick up your mat and walk." He might as well have told the stone columns to dance in a circle around the afflicted.

But something started to happen to the paralytic's muted nerve endings and shriveled limbs. Looking up at this unassuming stranger who spoke with such authority, the invalid struggled up onto his feet. Responding to the command of Christ, he found that the impossible became possible. Thirty-eight years of immobility faded away like a head cold.

Any other healer would have been content to just make a paralyzed man walk. That's a pretty good day's work—a deed glorious enough, in fact, for a lifetime. But Jesus had still more to say through this sign.

Tucked away in His simple statement that produced the miracle was a bomb that would detonate beneath the crusty pillars holding up the legalistic religion of His day. Jesus had commanded that the *man pick up his mat* and walk. And so the former invalid, bursting with gratitude and praise, walked off into the crowd of pilgrims going to the temple with his mat rolled up under his arm. The man probably hopped, skipped, and jumped his way through the crowd.

If ever there was a time to worship God on the Sabbath, this was it. So with his own loud praises he joined those celebrating. In his heart-thumping joy, the man did not realize that he was proclaiming himself a Sabbath breaker before the multitude of pilgrims around him. Jewish tradition clearly forbade any person to carry a mat on the Sabbath. That constituted "bearing a burden."

Word of this transgression reached the priests, and they promptly came to reprimand him. The former invalid explained that the One who healed him had told him to carry his mat. And here the religious leaders showed their true colors. An individual stood before them bubbling over with joy because thirty-eight years of humiliation and misery had just somersaulted inexplicably into perfect health. The man had been born again into a new body. But this marvelous deliverance paled into insignificance before the fact that the delivered man carried a mat under his arm.

They were not interested in his story. They wanted to know who had dared to give such a command and thereby cause this transgression of the Sabbath.

Jesus' bomb detonated before the multitude of pilgrims. The values of these guardians of the law were exposed. There was no room in their holy day for divine rescues; no room for the afflicted to be saved. Their Sabbath had become a fortress within which to defend tradition against all comers. This human being so dramatically touched by grace was invisible. They only noticed his inadvertent bump against the rules.

Jesus had one last brush stroke to make before his canvas was complete. He located the former paralytic in the temple and explained that deliverance should lead to reformation. In this case, the man's destructive lifestyle had contributed to his illness, and Jesus wanted to make sure he didn't fall into the same downward spiral again.

That afternoon, in a few moments by the pool of Bethesda, Jesus deftly sketched out a masterpiece. The centerpiece was just a few quick strokes of command: "Get up! Pick up your mat and walk." Bright basic colors against the grim walls, but how that act echoed!

The Master had drawn a lesson in faith surrounded by superstition. There were no paraphernalia attached to His healing; no grand gestures, no supernatural props to help legitimize the scene. Christ's act is so minimal one almost misses where the miracle occurs. For a crowd clinging desperately to a pool they invested with magical powers, He laid out a personal transaction. He made a statement; person-to-person, person-to-God is what counts, not person-to-object.

And His act of healing is also carefully composed as a model for spiritual salvation. We are utterly helpless in sin. Christ comes and introduces Himself. We have to want to be saved. He commands us to be whole. As we respond to Him in faith, we are made whole.

Finally, Jesus vividly contrasts His kingdom of grace with the dried-up religious establishment around Him.

Christ's acts have a precision and eloquence that makes people stand back and stare and study. They see beautiful qualities. His signs express so much. There's a wealth of meaning in this one scene painted for us by the pool of Bethesda. We can discover wonderful things to admire.

I believe a large part of our misery or our happiness in life will be determined by whether we develop this skill of admiring God. So instead of looking for someone to blame, invest time in looking for something about God to admire. Instead of manipulating and controlling people, invest emotional energy in just admiring. Instead of performing more or acquiring more, just admire. It can make all the difference. It can make all the difference even for those who grow up with holes in their hearts, as Jessica did.

Jessica's story, like the story of many women, begins with her father. She spent her childhood in a white, clapboard house on a dairy farm in Minnesota. It was an elegant Victorian home with hardwood floors and a stairway winding up all three stories. It could have been the place where a little girl whiled away the hours in innocent games and dreamed of a fairy-tale future.

But Jessica remembers living in fear much of the time. The worst of it was when her father came home drunk—and he came home drunk often.

One incident in particular stands out. She was playing in the screened back porch one fine spring day at the age of seven. A little sparrow had flown in through a tear in the screen, and Jessica watched fascinated as it fluttered around the porch, chirping loudly.

Then Bill, her father, stumbled up the steps, opened the screen door, and slammed it shut. The bird flew past his face and circled back behind him in its panic. He turned in his stupor and began swatting at it. The bird kept throwing itself against the screen until Bill grabbed in it his big palm. He seemed outraged at the sparrow's noisy chirping and suddenly pulled its head off.

Jessica shrieked in terror. Cowering on the porch, she pleaded, "Daddy, stop it, don't!"

The man threw the sparrow's body out into the yard then turned to his daughter and yelled, "You're gonna be next."

Jessica fled for her life through the screen door and around the house as Dad stumbled after her. She raced to the front porch and hid under its wooden slats. It was a cold, dark hiding place that had rescued her a number of times before.

It hadn't always been like that. Jessica's parents became Adventists when she was three years old. And her father tried his best to live an upright life, to live up to all the church's standards. He was a rather poor Minnesota farmer, but one day he vowed to start paying a double tithe. And Bill kept his promise.

Not long afterward, however, something happened at a church social that deeply hurt the man. The church treasurer's brother walked up to Bill and accused him, in front of other church members, of not paying an honest tithe.

Bill called to his family and walked straight out of that gathering. On the way home, he vowed never to step inside an Adventist church again. He kept that promise, too, for many years.

Bill became a very bitter, angry man. He just couldn't get over this public questioning of his uprightness—after all he'd invested in upholding the standards. So he took up the bottle with a vengeance and began to take out his pain and frustration on his wife and daughters. They had refused to leave the church, and he regarded this as a kind of betrayal.

Jessica remembers a lot of screaming and cursing. Sometimes in a drunken rage Bill would even threaten his family with a revolver.

Jessica's mother tried her best to raise her daughters as Adventists, but Bill wouldn't permit her to conduct family worships. They had to pray silently.

Many nights, Jessica fell asleep in silent prayer. She wanted to believe that there was a God up there who cared for her, but it was hard.

One evening, Jessica noticed her mother peering out the kitchen window looking very worried. Bill had been gone all day, and it was long past suppertime. For some reason, on this night, Jessica's mother spoke the fear that she always kept hidden away: "I hope your Daddy's not going to come home drunk again."

Jessica walked out to the front yard and knelt down on the grass. With the earnest, spontaneous faith of a child, she folded her hands and prayed, "Please don't let my daddy come home drunk."

But several hours later, Bill came through the front door, red-faced and bleary-eyed.

Jessica's faith was shattered. How could she trust God after that?

It was hard enough when Sabbath School teachers urged her to just talk to God "as if he were your father." That didn't make any sense at all.

Even some of the most tender images in the Bible filled her with dread. When she read the text about God knowing when every sparrow falls, Jessica couldn't help thinking of that terrifying scene on the back porch.

People told Jessica that she was a child of the king, but she could never quite believe that she was worthy of such an honor. Surely that sort of thing was for other people.

At home, Jessica felt she was walking a tightrope. She wanted to please her loving, godly mother and do the things a good Adventist girl did. But she craved her father's love. And he kept wanting to turn her in the opposite direction, trying to get her to take a few puffs of his cigarettes, for example, as a way of snubbing his nose at the church.

Jessica felt as if she could never quite fit in—anywhere. In high school she was afraid to invite friends over to her house. Who knew what might happen when father came home? She dreaded the day some boy she liked might find out her dad was an alcoholic. Jessica had her little speech all prepared: "It's OK, you don't have to date me anymore."

Jessica grew up as a broken person, feeling incomplete and rejected. She could very easily have rejected God altogether. She could very easily have tried to drown her pain in drugs or promiscuity. Or she could very easily have sunk into the religion of avoidance, the religion of having to be right, the religion of manipulation—all the twisted ways that dysfunctional people try to earn that acceptance and love they so desperately need.

But Jessica didn't. She didn't fall into these ruts. By some miracle of grace, she began to invest herself in relationships.

It started after her mother enrolled her in an Adventist academy. During her senior year Jessica began to realize that all the talk in chapel about "a personal relationship with Jesus Christ" was starting to sink in a bit. That message often was distorted by the legalism of several faculty members—a religion teacher who grew livid when kids joked around in pig latin; that seemed just a step short of the dreaded speaking in tongues; a history teacher who passionately affirmed that high heels were sexually suggestive. But grace somehow seeped in anyway.

Jessica discovered some genuine friendships at the academy, kids who seemed to love her for who she was, who weren't put off by her miserable home life, who stuck with her through thick and thin. Some of the Adventist parents who knew about Jessica's alcoholic father even encouraged their children to befriend her.

This was a new experience.

Jessica decided to start praying for her father again. Her mother had always encouraged her to do so, but after years of seeing him decay in his alcoholism, she'd given up. He wasn't ever going to change. Now, however, something made her more hopeful.

As she began praying for Dad, she began pleading for herself too. Jessica desperately wanted to have a Christian home; she didn't want her kids growing up the way she had. But how do you become a good wife and mother? Jessica feared she couldn't pull it off. She started depending on God to choose someone for her who could help create a different home life.

And that year she began dating Ron. He came from a warm Christian home and had developed his own friendship with Jesus. His prayers were so natural, so spontaneous. It was obvious that Jesus was really there for Ron. He wasn't at all showy about his religious faith. He just exhibited qualities that Jessica deeply admired.

Jessica and Ron went to different Adventist colleges but kept in touch through phone calls and letters. In her freshman Bible class, Jessica was assigned to read *The Desire of Ages*. Before, she'd always studied just to get good grades. But now something in this book about Jesus' life and ministry captivated her. He came alive as a real person. Scenes from the gospels made Him so approachable, so trustworthy.

For the first time in her life, this young woman could simply invest herself in admiring Jesus. He was worth getting to know. She could open up to Him. Jessica started praying out loud. Memories of her father's prohibitions had made that impossible before. Her old fears were dropping away. She began to actually feel what a father's love might really be like. She started falling in love with Jesus.

Ron's phone calls reinforced this experience. Their conversation across thousands of miles was growing more intimate and tender. That's the way prayer could be! Ron began writing Jessica love letters every day. That's what the Bible really is, Jessica realized, God's love letter to me!

This young woman began reading the Bible regularly for the first time. It was slow and sporadic at first. She was still haunted by the painful experiences of her childhood. But she kept investing her thoughts and feelings in the picture of Jesus painted in the gospels. She invested herself in listening to the words of grace and encouragement in the epistles—and taking them to heart. Yes, she was a child of the king. Yes, she belonged. Yes, she was accepted.

Today Jessica and Ron have a wonderful Christian ministry together. And they've established a Christian home. They begin every morning opening the drapes in their bedroom to let the sunlight flood in. Then they cuddle in bed and have a time of conversational prayer. It's something that Jessica especially delights in after all the years of silence in her home.

Jessica has had her struggles with fear and insecurity. It took her a long, long time to be able to pray in public. It took her a long time to be able to rest in the arms of a heavenly Father. But she invested herself in the right things. She didn't invest herself in performing more, in appearing more upright than someone else, in being right and making others wrong, in trying to control someone else and make them give her the love she needed.

Jessica began to admire Jesus. She persisted. She invested herself in a relationship with Him until she began to experience His love and grace.

Today Jessica says, "Jesus is my best friend. I make that friendship my top priority. I've been so fragile most of my life, something like a cracked pot. But I've learned that God can use all our pain and disappointments. He can let His light shine through the cracks. The glue that has held this cracked pot together is Isaiah 43:1-5:

> 'Fear not, for I have redeemed you;
> I have summoned you by name; you are mine.' "

Things have come full circle for Jessica. One day she received news that her father, at the age of 56, had "given his heart to Jesus." It seemed a sudden, inexplicable change. He'd even begun having evening worship with Mother in that three-story Victorian house. Apparently their prayers had been answered at last.

During her next visit home, Jessica sat on the back porch with her dad and asked him what had happened.

It was the local Adventist pastor, he said. The man had come over to sit a spell on this very porch and chatted, just like a good neighbor might do. Bill had been very noncommunicative at first. He just sat there looking out as dusk settled over the meadows. But the pastor kept coming, and once in a while he and Dad would go to a ball game. He gave Bill the idea that maybe— just maybe—all Christians weren't judgmental.

One day, Bill took a short walk through the pasture toward the woods, swinging a bottle of whiskey in his hand. Suddenly he looked up into the sky and told God, "This is the last drink I'll ever take."

He threw the bottle away and kept his promise.

When Jessica asked her father how he'd gotten to the point of opening his heart to God, he thought a moment and then said a lot of it had to do with forgiving the man who'd offended him so many years ago. He had to let God deal with the bitterness in his heart.

A few weeks later, Jessica was able to fly back home for a long visit with her parents. She and Bill sat on the back porch a lot. He opened up about things in his own life, about the time his older brothers got him drunk when he was five just to see him stumble around, about the mother who'd been unable to express affection. Bill had always found it difficult to express his own feelings. But now, staring out at dusk through the screened porch, he talked about the peace and forgiveness he'd found at last.

Bill had become a gentle, humble man who treated Mother like a queen. They enjoyed studying the Bible together now. The yelling and the drinking seemed a distant nightmare.

Two years later, Bill died of cancer. But Jessica had come to know what God's love can really do, what prayer can really do. So many people had persisted in prayer on Bill's behalf. She had been given a father back. And she finally heard the words, at the age of twenty-nine, that every little girl growing up needs to hear.

It happened when Bill called to break the news about his illness. Jessica started crying and told her dad that she loved him.

And for the first time, Bill said it back, in a quivering voice, "I love you too."

Jessica says now, "I'm so thankful that God gave me a little glimpse of Himself by letting me have a short relationship with father before he died, the kind of relationship I'd always dreamed of."

Love brings healing to broken people. Love can bring wholeness to the compulsive and the controlling. Love creates healthy human beings. Love creates healthy religion.

There's no substitute. There's no other substance with which we can build spirituality. Everything else is a counterfeit. Everything else eventually burns us out. There's only one way into the Christian life. And that's the way of love.

It begins—and ends—with simply admiring the Christ who cherishes us.